BIT BY BIT

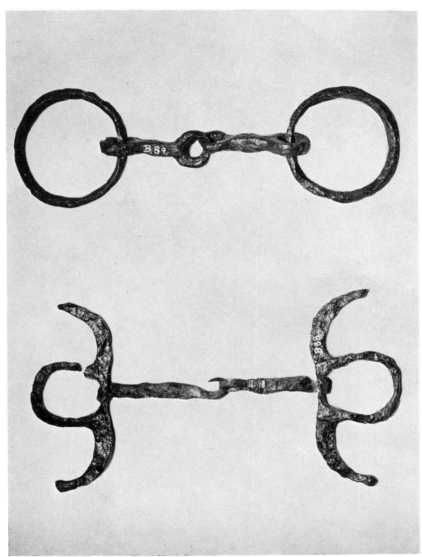

FIRST CENTURY ROMAN BIT

The equine bit dates back to very early days, when man first made the horse his servant. Bits were simple, but remarkably like those in use today.

BIT BY BIT

A GUIDE TO EQUINE BITS

by

DIANA TUKE

ILLUSTRATED WITH
PHOTOGRAPHS BY
DONALD TUKE

J. A. ALLEN & CO. LTD.

LONDON

Dedicated to the Animal Health Trust's equine research
station at Balaton Lodge, Newmarket, in recognition of their
tireless work to conquer equine ills and injuries.

First published 1965
Reprinted 1969
Reprinted 1972
Reprinted 1975
Reprinted 1979
Reprinted 1985

ISBN 0-85131-033-8
© Diana R. Tuke, 1965

Published by
J. A. Allen & Company Limited,
1, Lower Grosvenor Place,
Buckingham Palace Road,
London, SW1W 0EL.

Reprinted and bound by
Butler & Tanner Limited, Frome, Somerset

CONTENTS

ACKNOWLEDGEMENTS

ACKNOWLEDGEMENTS and grateful thanks are due to the following.

The Animal Health Trust's equine research station at Balaton Lodge, Newmarket, Suffolk, for supplying the X-ray photograph.

The Pony Club.

Lieut.-Colonel J. F. S. Bullen and Miss Jennie Bullen of The Catherston Stud, The Manor House, Didmarton, Gloucestershire, for the bits in figs. 127, 128 and 152.

The Corinium Museum, Cirencester, Gloucestershire, for permission to photograph the Roman bits. Fig. 20.

The directors and staff of Messrs. F. E. Gibson Ltd., Saddlers, Sales Paddock Lane, Newmarket, Suffolk, who have been most helpful and put their entire stock of bits at my disposal.

Lieut.-Colonel P. E. Langford, of the School of Infantry, Warminster, Wiltshire, for the loan of his Jodhphur polo curb chain.

Messrs. Moss, Stone and Co. Ltd., of the Eldonian Works, Bath Street, Walsall, Staffordshire, for their help in Chapter One, and for letting us photograph the foundry in action and a large number of bits that were still missing from the collection.

Mr. W. Seaman, M.H., joint-master of the North Norfolk Harriers, and his wife, and their daughter Jane, of Grange Farm, Erpingham, Norwich, Norfolk, for their help in Chapter Five. They provided the two bits (figs. 169 and 176) and leather curb chain (fig. 164), and also the horses. Readers of *A Long Road to Harringay* will remember the little chestnut mare, Gold Charm. It is under her real name that she appears in this book, and I am grateful to Jane and her parents for letting me use Castania. As always, she entered into the spirit of the show and gave of her best, patiently accepting the many different bits as they were slipped in and out of her mouth. It meant a great deal to me to have her in this book.

Captain F. Spicer, D.S.O., of Spye Park, Chippenham, Wiltshire, for kindly loaning some of the rarer bits, one of which was a genuine "Latchford" (fig. 160). Figs. 70, 159, 160.

My brother Donald who undertook all the photography for the book.

D.R.T.

ILLUSTRATIONS

CHAPTER FOUR

CHAPTER FIVE

CHAPTER SIX

CONCLUSION

By the same author

STITCH BY STITCH
A Guide to Equine Saddles

HORSE BY HORSE
A Guide to Equine Care & Management

GETTING YOUR HORSE FIT

THE RIDERS HANDBOOK

PREFACE

EVER since my early childhood, saddler's shops have held for me an unexplainable fascination. I could then, and still can, spend hours just quietly browsing in the hope that I will discover something new (fig. 1). With the years, during which I struggled to understand books, written for adults and far beyond me, on equitation and horsemastership, my childish curiosity turned to a real desire to learn and understand. There is so much more to riding and horses than merely getting on to them and going for a ride. For if we are to obtain the fullest enjoyment from this pastime and become true horsemen and women, then we must study saddlery in its widest sense. It is an extremely interesting subject, for it is thanks to our enterprising saddlers that we have our first-class saddles. But saddles alone are no good to us if we do not know something about the equally interesting and important subject – bits and bitting. If we do not know something about the art of good and sound bitting, and the many different bits that there are to choose from, we will never do justice to our saddles, let alone our horses.

To me, at first, bits were just bits. I accepted them as such. There were three definite, different types and that was all. Then, when Castania came to me, backed but unschooled, a 4-year-old straight from weaning her first foal, I realized that if I was to succeed in schooling her myself I would really have to study the subject. Otherwise I would not know what I was putting in her mouth and be quite incapable of getting the best out of her.

I owe my first practical knowledge on the subject of bitting to our own saddler in Dulverton, the late Mr. S. J. Vickery. His wide knowledge and experience helped me to bit Castania correctly and to overcome her tricks. It was in Mr. Vickery's shop that I first saw Market Harboroughs. He had been commissioned to make them for the Olympic team of 1952 in training at Porlock, and kindly showed them to me before sending them over to Captain Collings. Two years later, I went to Porlock myself, for the last three weeks of the fifteen-week horsemastership course, to gain my B.H.S. certificate. It was while I was there that the stud groom, giving us a lecture on bits and bitting, roused my interest in the subject. It was he, explaining how a snaffle can vary in its severity according to the shape of the arms and tightness of the joint, that sparked it off. To the late Captain Tony Collings' stud groom, Mr. M. Ffitch, M.M., who was still in office the winter following the tragic death of Captain Collings, when Major Paddy Burke had taken over the running of Porlock, I am most indebted.

Though I have covered an extensive number of bits, I do not for one moment pretend to have covered them all. It would have been neither possible, nor a sound policy. Some bits are best left unrecorded, and others are so outdated as to be fit only for museum pieces. All the same, I have tried to cover most of the bits in present-day use and a few of those that might still be around in old-established stables. I hope, therefore, that having read this book the reader will be a little clearer about the important art of bitting.

When I finished this book in mid-September, little did we know that before the year was out Castania would be ours again. She returned to our family for good on December 2nd, thereby bringing true the last sentence of *A Long Road to Harringay*.

Summer, 1964   D.R.T.

Fig. 1. A Saddler's shop

CHAPTER ONE

FROM MOULD TO MOUTH —
HOW MODERN BITS ARE MADE

BEFORE passing to the various different aspects of the bits themselves, it is interesting to realize how they are made. For this gives us a truer picture of the subject and enables us to appreciate the finer points of each bit.

In the past, bits were hand forged by craftsmen whose numbers have steadily dwindled over the years. The art and scope of the loriner in those days was considerable. He made his bits to his customer's specific requirements without undue regard to either the time or the effort involved. Hand-forged bits are now rare; in their place we have cast bits made by foundrymen. The range of bits any one firm can hold is, by necessity of cost, limited. The master pattern used in casting is expensive, so few manufacturers can afford to hold patterns that are not in demand. In special cases they will have one modelled if the customer makes the number of bits from such a moulding worth while. To make a master pattern for one bit would be ludicrous, but if the customer agreed to having a few dozen such bits, then it would be a reasonable proposition. In fact, the bit in fig. 2 is one from a special order for a private customer in the United States. Walking horse bits vary in design and each individual has his own favourite; as we do in this country. Nevertheless, as will be seen later in this book, the range of bits available today is more than adequate, so the need for having a special bit made to order is seldom necessary.

Bit making is a lengthy business, employing much hand work. It is no good expecting a saddler to obtain a bit which is temporarily out of stock, both in his shop and the manufacturer's stockroom, in under six to eight weeks. This is the time needed from mould to mouth.

Steel, which used to be the bane of a groom's life, has now been replaced by stainless steel. Renowned for its toughness and resistance to corrosion, it is an ideal material. Not only is it malleable, which helps in manufacturing the bits, but it also carries a high lustre, reducing the need to polish it after every outing. A thorough washing to remove all marks and saliva, followed by a quick rub on a clean stable rubber, is all that is required between routine polishings to keep them in good condition. This, for the owner-groom, is a genuine saving of time.

This book is not long enough to allow for more than a condensed picture of the process of casting, but I will do my best to outline the procedure.

Casting is the most direct method by which small quantities of a given shape can be produced. The process consists essentially of pouring metal into a destructible sand-mould. Before the moulds can be made, a master pattern has to be modelled and this is by far the most expensive part both in time and money. Not only must the master pattern be dimensionally accurate (with allowance made for the contraction of the metal when it cools and the removal of some metal in grinding and polishing, so that patterns are made fractionally larger than the finished article), but full consideration must also be given to making it meet the foundry's requirements.

The master pattern made, the next stage is the production of the mould itself. These, too, have to be dimensionally accurate and sufficiently stable to permit the metal to solidify into the exact shape of the mould cavity.

In the case of castings which are designed with overhanging flanges, ringholes and hollowed out sections, straightforward moulds are no good owing to their irregularity of shape. A great many bits come into this category, and to overcome the problem the foundryman has to resort to using small cores which correspond with the shape of the irregularity. Cores are made by simply ramming sand mixed with linseed oil and binder into a box (fig. 3), and then baking the whole shape hard till it forms a solid mass that breaks up easily when the molten metal cools and contracts on solidification. These cores are then used in the moulds.

There are two types of moulds, the wooden flask or stump mould (fig. 6) and the steel frame or tub mould (fig. 7). Both types are large enough to provide several inches of sand all round the patterns and the channels which carry the metal to the mould cavities during filling. In order to be able to remove the master pattern (fig. 4), the moulds are made in two halves by ramming in sand till it is hard and capable of self-support. The patterns are then removed, and pouring holes carved in the top side to allow filling. Cores are fitted in the required places and the two halves closed together on a wooden board, and placed on the foundry floor ready to receive the molten metal.

While the moulds have been in the process of construction, the electric furnace has been melting the stainless steel. This is poured (fig. 5) into a pre-heated crucible capable of holding fifty pounds of metal, and carried by two men in a steel frame called a shank. The liquid white metal is poured through the hole in the top of the moulds and into the cavities left by the patterns (figs. 6 and 7).

After a brief period the metal has solidified sufficiently to allow the moulds to be broken open and the still red-hot castings removed (fig. 8). These are allowed to cool to room temperature before being either broken or cut off from the thick channels to which they are attached. As only about 40 per cent of the metal poured in is actually used in the castings themselves, the remainder, in the form of channels and pouring nozzles, is returned to the furnace for re-melting.

We have now obtained the various parts of the bits (fig. 9), but there is still a great deal of work to be done before they can even be assembled. First, the surplus sand is either shot-blasted off or removed in a tumbler barrel. Then the surplus metal is ground off and the castings returned to another tumbler barrel containing oil and emery, where they remain for a period of days. This process removes all the rough scale from the surface of the casting and leaves it with a smooth, dull lustre. While in the barrel, advantage is taken of polishing the inside of closed sections by fitting, where possible, steel rings. This greatly reduces costs later on.

The castings are now ready to pass on to the machining and assembly shops. In order to have as wide a range of sizes as possible, the bit is made in several parts (fig. 10), and then assembled by hand. Any one bit can have big rings or small, or long cheeks or short, fitted to one of several different mouth widths and shapes. When an order comes in, providing there is a stock of parts to meet the order, the correct ring or cheek size and shape is selected and, along with the type of mouth required, sent to the assembly shop. This work is all done by hand and calls for a high degree of accuracy, for no latitude is possible if the fitting and standard of bits is to be maintained. First, the inside of each part is cleaned and prepared (figs. 11 and 12), then it is fitted to its component ready for joining. This is done in several ways according to the type of mouth and cheek. With Weymouths and Pelhams, the mouthpiece ends are heated and then forged round the beam of the cheek to form a neat joint which is welded (fig. 13). In the case of fixed mouthpieces, the ends are riveted before welding. Jointed bits, on the other hand, are knocked together cold (fig. 14), and then welded.

Eggbutt snaffles have their own problems, which apply to the Dee snaffles as well. Here, before joining the mouthpiece to the rings, small brass bushes, which are made on a special machine (fig. 15), have to be inserted into the necks of each to ensure free movement of the rings and prevent wear (fig. 16). Once these are in place the holes are cleared by drilling (fig. 17), the C-shaped rings fitted and a rod passed through the whole and the ends riveted. The rivets are then welded over. This particular method of making eggbutt snaffles has been carried out with success by this firm for several years, but it is not universal.

The bit now looks like a bit and not just an odd piece of casting. It is, in fact, complete save for the polishing. In the case of fixed-mouth bits, some preliminary polishing is done before assembly, but in every case they all pass on to the polishing shop. The polishing of a bit requires much hard work to remove the imperfections left by the previous operations. This is done by pressing the surfaces of the metal against various grades of rotating emery belts in order of increasing fineness. A banding machine (fig. 18) is used for the inside of the rings and things like stirrup irons where the surface is on the inside. The bits then pass to the final stages (fig. 19). First, the sisal mop covered with a fine layer of polishing grease, which adds a dull lustre to the now smooth surface; then, having been immersed in lime, the leather mop for colouring off, which gives a bright mirror finish.

Even so, the bits are not yet ready to leave the foundry. The final polishing done, they are now subject to a series of inspections for flaws and surface imperfections in order to maintain a high standard of finish. In some instances the rejection rate is fairly high, especially so when the mouthpiece of the bit is hollow and the metal thickness is small in order to reduce the weight of the bit. For this reason the price of a hollow mouth bit is higher than that for a solid mouth one of the same design, but it is well worth it.

Naturally, this is only a quick look at a lengthy process and a highly-skilled job, but I hope I have conveyed a little of the work that goes into producing our bits today, before we, the riders, even see, let alone use them.

Fig. 2. A special order – American walking horse bit.

Fig. 3. Sand cores being made.

Fig. 4. Master pattern in stump mould.

Fig. 5. Stainless steel being poured into crucible.

Fig. 6. Stump moulds being filled.

Fig. 7. Tub moulds being filled.

8

9

10

11

12

13

Fig.   8. Removing castings from tub mould.
Fig.   9. Rough castings after being broken off.
Fig. 10. Bit parts awaiting assembly.
Fig. 11. Filing inside eye of Pelham cheek (preparing bits).
Fig. 12. Grinding end of mouthpiece (preparing bits).
Fig. 13. Forging mouthpiece to cheek.

Fig. 14. Joining a jointed mouthpiece.
Fig. 16. Putting in the brass bushes.
Fig. 18. The banding machine.

Fig. 15. Making brass bushes.
Fig. 17. Drilling to clear the holes.
Fig. 19. The final stages – polishing.

CHAPTER TWO

AN INTRODUCTION TO THE ART OF BITTING

THE equine bit dates back to very early days, when man first made the horse his servant. In those far off times, bits were simple and remarkably like those in use today (Frontispiece and fig. 20). Gradually, through the centuries, they developed into much more complicated affairs, until by the Tudors they had become very ornate – horrific curbs with long cheeks and sharp action. These bits, luckily for the horse, went out of vogue in the centuries that followed and reverted slowly to a simpler form, until, today, the range available is less comprehensive than it was even a century ago. Nevertheless, the choice of bits is still extensive and a wide variety are still in use, with each one varying to some degree from its counterpart.

To the ordinary horseman, bits of the same group probably look alike. But this is far from being the case. To get the best out of our horses we must consider the advantages and disadvantages of each group of bits, and of bits within a group, before finally deciding which one we are going to use. The foremost consideration is the comfort of the horse. If the horse is not comfortable about his head he will fret and we, in turn, will have an uncomfortable ride. It behoves us, therefore, to give a little thought to this question before rushing off to buy the first bit we like the look of. Ten to one it will be unsuitable and quite useless for the job required of it.

Bits can, for convenience, be divided into three main groups – snaffle, double and Pelham. Though I know most people would divide them into more groups, I prefer to use three groups and sub-divide the groups afterwards, for in this way we keep bits of a similar make-up under the same main group, which makes identification and explanation that much easier.

A bit consists of anything passing through a horse's mouth, and then, by way of the reins, to the rider's hands. The simplest bit of all is probably that used by the North American Indians, a piece of rawhide, which after all is a snaffle. In South America, too, we find the Bocado bit; this is first cousin to the North American one, being a piece of rawhide 2 feet long which is passed through the horse's mouth, under the tongue, and tied under the lower jaw.

A horse's mouth is quite as, if not more, sensitive than our own, therefore care must be taken not to damage or injure the parts of the mouth and head that come in contact with the bit and bridle. Once damage has been caused its effects are very hard to remedy. The only course left open may be to use a stronger bit, and when this, in many cases through causing more pain, fails to answer the rider has to revert to a very soft bit with some other aid to control the horse, or even a bitless bridle. In principle, the use of a stronger bit is wrong; no horse is born with a really bad mouth. Bad mouths are made by careless rough riding and handling, coupled with thoughtless bitting, seldom by heredity. Only in the hands of an expert, with a calm temperament and light hands, can a strong bit be condoned. Never in the hands of a young child or inexperienced rider; and least of all in the hands of a rider who has little control over his or her temper!

Today we have several different materials to choose from for the mouthpieces of our bits: rubber and vulcanite, which are both very easy and soft on the mouth, metal of various kinds, and in some cases even wood and leather. But the former three are the most usual and are to be found in a wide variety of mouthpieces, mullen (half-moon) and jointed.

It is true to say that the thinner the mouthpiece, the sharper the action. This is why, very often, a horse will go kindly in a bit with a fat mouthpiece (fig. 21), but fret badly in a thin one, like a racing snaffle (fig. 22), which may be cutting into the sensitive bars of its mouth. This also applies to the use of thin bridoon on its own (fig. 23), without an accompanying curb bit, as sometimes seen on children's ponies. It is used in the mistaken assumption that the thinner bit is lighter and therefore more likely to be kinder – in fact it is the reverse, it is far sharper and more dangerous. For this reason it is always wise to choose a bit with a reasonably thick mouthpiece. No good has ever come from inflicting pain on a horse; they always fight against it and win in the end.

Another point to consider, before choosing a bit, besides our own ability as a rider (a very important factor), is the conformation of the horse's mouth, as no two are alike. A well-bred horse will very often, though not always, have a long thin mouth giving ample room for the bit. These horses are eminently suited to either a snaffle, with or without a drop noseband, or a double bridle, but will be found hard to fit with a Pelham. The reason for this is the fact that a long mouth allows the bit, when properly adjusted so that it rests lightly and snugly against the corners of the mouth (fig. 24), to ride too high in the mouth, and, in consequence, the curb-chain rides up out of its correct place and acts on the outer jaw-bones instead of the curb groove (fig. 25). On the other hand, a horse of more common lineage will be found to have a fatter, shorter mouth with little or no room for two bits. These horses, though suited to an ordinary snaffle, are quite unsuited to either a drop noseband or double bridle, but will be found to go extremely well in a Pelham. In fact they are the only type that can be said to warrant a Pelham.

Lastly, we come to the teeth, which play an important part in the bitting and comfort of the horse. In the case of a stallion or gelding (and in very rare cases a mare), once mature, they will have, besides their other teeth, four spike-like teeth (two on each jaw), similar to the canine teeth in a dog; these are called tushes and lie to the rear of the front teeth, on the outer edges of the jaw before it narrows to form the bars. Owing to their position they cut down the space available for a bit and, in a short-mouthed horse, this can cause a definite bitting problem, as the bit is inclined to rattle against them and cause annoyance. Wolf-teeth, too, can be a source of trouble. These are rudimentary teeth that occur sometimes in front of the back molars, on either side of the jaw, especially the top jaw. Besides being very painful when cut they also interfere with the bit and can cause a great deal of trouble and fretting. In the author's opinion,

like ones own wisdom teeth, they are best removed. But remember, this is strictly a
job for a veterinary surgeon and must only be done on his advice.

Before leaving the subject of teeth—the cause of so much trouble both eating and
biting—I would like to remind readers of the absolute necessity to have their horses'
teeth examined regularly to ascertain whether or not the back molars need filing. This
applies to horses of all ages, and is a very simple job in the hands of a veterinary surgeon.
The necessity to file back molars lies in the fact that the upper jaw is wider than the
lower one, and the upper molars grow downwards and outwards, whereas the lower
ones grow upwards and inwards. The result is that the outer edge of the upper molars
and the inner edge of the lower ones receive virtually no wear, becoming extremely
sharp. Once sharp they can lacerate the cheeks and tongue, to the extent that the horse
fights shy of its bit and is unable to eat its food. So do be warned, and if in doubt call in
your veterinary surgeon, it is well worth it.

By placing a bridle and bit on a horse we bring into play one or more of the seven
points of control we have at our disposal. These are, in fact, points of pressure and each
one of them is extremely sensitive unless damaged. First and foremost comes the tongue.
This can be large or small, fine or coarse, and takes all or some of the pressure with
every form of bit except the Bocado, and maybe one with a very high, wide port. On
either side of the tongue lie the bars. These are the flesh-covered jaw bones minus
teeth, and divide the front teeth from the back ones. The layer of flesh that covers the
bars is very sensitive and varies in thickness according to the breeding of the horse: a
well-bred horse having a much thinner, and therefore more sensitive, layer than his
more common cousin. The latter's mouth can be so well endowed with flesh that he
hardly feels the bit pressing on the bars, but this does not necessarily mean that it has a
hard mouth, merely a less sensitive one. Next comes the lips, which not only regulate
the height of the bit but also its width. A bit must fit easily and snugly and be neither too
wide nor too narrow for the mouth, as the extremely thin, tender skin that covers the
corners of the lips is easily damaged and cut. The lips suffer a lot from the rider with
rough hands, and care must be taken not to saw on the bit for the reason that once cut
they take a long time to heal, and can cause a great deal of discomfort and trouble.
Directly behind the lower jaw bones, above the lower lip, lies the curb-groove through
which, by means of a curb chain, we obtain flexion. Moving upwards, we come to the
next point of pressure and control, the poll. When pressure is brought to bear in any
degree, it has a lowering effect on the horse's head. This effect can be obtained by either
a curb or by means of an overhead check rein. In either case care must be taken not to
use force or violence, for, lying as it does at the junction of the skull and vertebrae of
the neck, the poll is in close proximity to the brain, rendering it extremely vulnerable.
A sudden jerk on a curb rein or overhead check could result in injury of a lasting
nature, but gentle pressure is quite harmless, rendering a curb bit in experienced hands
a perfectly safe and sound bit.

Though not in direct contact with the bit the nose plays an important part in
bitting. In recent years much more use has been made of the noseband in some form or
other. At one time they were rarely seen, but returned to fashion during this century.
With careful use of some nosebands a rider can induce a certain amount of flexion, and

bring his horse's head into the correct position without resorting to a curb bit. The most widely used and principle one is the drop noseband. Great care must be exercised in fitting it correctly. So often one sees a drop noseband with the front resting on the edge of the nostril flaps and buckled tightly round the mouth. This is both incorrect and dangerous, as it interferes with the horse's breathing. The drop refers not to the whole noseband, but only to the back strap which passes below the snaffle bit to fasten in the curb-groove, leaving room for the horse to mouth. Correctly fitted (fig. 26), a drop noseband is a useful addition for it enables a rider to school a horse to a greater degree without having to use a double bridle too soon. It also helps to prevent a horse from crossing its jaws and catching hold of the bit in its teeth (a nasty habit of the long-mouthed horse), and at the same time helps to keep the mouth moist, which is essential if a soft mouth is to be maintained. On no account should a drop noseband be used with a curb bit and chain, as this combination relies on the horse being free to open its mouth and relax its jaw. Another noseband employing the nose by direct contact with the bit is the Kineton or Puckle noseband, so called after Mr. Puckle of Kineton. It passes by way of metal loops round either side of the mouthpiece inside the snaffle rings, ensuring that, when contact is made with the bit, pressure is brought on the nose as well. Like the drop noseband it must only be used with a snaffle; and in the hands of an experienced rider it is excellent on a puller. Closely akin to this combination come three bridles which all employ a noseband fixed to the bit, the Newmarket, the Norton Perfection (fig. 27), and the Rockwell snaffle (fig. 28).

Lastly, we come to the seventh point of pressure and contact, the roof of the mouth. Nowadays, owing to the high-ported bit having gone out of fashion, mercifully for the horse, it is a point seldom used. When a high-port was tipped forward and the curb rein was used, the port pressed against the roof of the mouth and forced it open. It was like jacking the mouth open with a wedge. A nasty method indeed, and much the cruellest action of a curb. The only time it might come into action is if a moderate port is used and the cavesson noseband is adjusted low and buckled tightly round the jaw. This would prevent the horse opening its mouth and the port might touch it. It is a practice not to be recommended, and the reason why a drop noseband should never be used with a curb.

For a truer picture of what lies beneath the seven points of pressure a study of figs. 29 and 30 is a help. With the latter it is possible to see what lies hidden from the human eye, and just what parts of the horse's head we are inflicting pressure on, before we choose a bit.

Even so, whatever bit the rider ultimately chooses rests largely with the horse's temperament, stage of training, and the rider's own personal preference. It is always well to remember that in nine cases out of ten it is the gentle, soft bit that will give the best results. Above all, a horse must be comfortable to be in control; that is the secret of the art of good bitting.

Fig. 20. First-century Roman bits.
Fig. 22. A thin racing snaffle.
Fig. 24. Adjusted to rest lightly against the corners.

Fig. 21. A fat mouthpiece
Fig. 23. A thin bridoon.
Fig. 25. Rides up and acts on the outer jaw-bones.

26

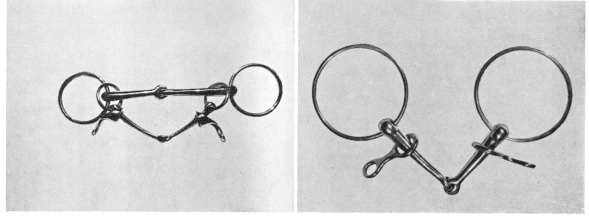

27

28

Fig. 26. A correctly fitted drop noseband is a
useful asset.

Fig. 27. The Norton Perfection. Improved
pattern.

Fig. 28. Rockwell snaffle bridle.

Fig. 29. Head study for seven points of control.

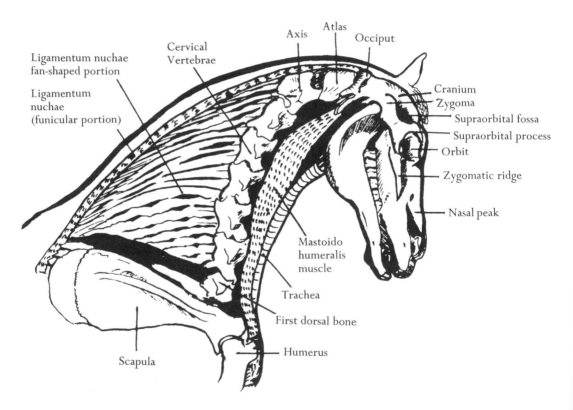

Fig. 30. An anatomical study – what lies hidden from the human eye. (*Professor R. H. Smythe.*)

CHAPTER THREE

BITS are like a tree. The main trunk represents the means by which we control our mount and regulate its pace. The trunk then splits into three, our three groups, snaffle, double, and Pelham. From these the tree branches and re-branches to give us many variations on the same theme.

The snaffle heads in importance and is probably the largest. The word snaffle comes, according to the Oxford dictionary, from the Dutch, snavel, and the German, schnabel, and means to mouth or break, hence the reason it was given to this type of bit. The snaffle, according to the rider's hands, acts on the tongue, bars or sides of the bars in the case of a jointed bit, the lips and the corners of the mouth. The group can be sub-divided in those snaffles which have either a straight mouth, mullen mouth or jointed mouth in their many guises. These are classed as snaffles to the ordinary layman. Next we have the gag, which is first cousin to the ordinary snaffle, save for the fact that it runs on the cheek piece and acts on the corners of the mouth and, to a certain extent, the poll. The last of these sub-groups covers the many specialist snaffles and breaking bits.

When choosing a snaffle thought must be given to the amount of severity we need. As I have remarked earlier, the thicker the mouthpiece, the gentler the action, owing to the greater bearing surface afforded on the bars, whereas a thin snaffle, for the reverse reason, will be found to be very sharp as it cuts into the sensitive nerves lying directly below the thin skin covering the bars. Of all the snaffles, the straight bar and mullen mouthpieces are the kindest, especially if covered in either rubber or vulcanite. Leather, too, is sometimes used for the reason that it is soft.

After these, come the many jointed snaffles. Their mouthpieces vary in severity very considerably, depending on two important factors other than the size of the mouthpiece – the shape of the arms and the looseness of the joint; points that must be remembered and taken into account when selecting a bit of this kind. The greater the curve of the arms and the tighter the joint, the less sharp the nutcracker action on the tongue; while a straight-armed mouthpiece coupled with a very loose joint will be found to be extremely sharp as the two arms can exert a much greater pinching of the tongue. The ideal is a bit with a loose joint that cannot close too much. This ensures that the horse can play with the bit and at the same time his tongue will not get unduly pinched. An excellent example of the straight arm is to be found with the Scorrier (fig. 71), which for some reason has grown in popularity. Owing to its make-up, it is, in fact, one of the severest snaffles on the market and should only be used by the even-tempered, competent horseman or woman; and never, under any circumstances, by a novice or child. This also applies to the many twisted mouthpieces, because being rough they can cause great pain and, in the hands of the inexperienced or rough rider, much damage.

It will be noticed that some snaffles have either flat or round (known as wire) rings, with or without eggbutt sides, while others have long cheeks. The object of the eggbutt side is to prevent rubbing and pinching of the lips, while the latter also doing this, helps to keep the bit evenly placed in the mouth and prevents it from being pulled through the mouth, which sometimes is the case with small rings. Extra-large rings are also adopted for this reason and are used on race horses. The advantage of the wire or round ring over a flat ring is that the former requires a smaller hole in the bit and is less likely to wear a rough edge, as is the case with the latter when they have been in use for some time. Once this happens a sore mouth quickly follows. The long cheek has the added advantage, too, of giving gentle cheek pressure on the sides of the horse's face, this, with some horses, is a great help in keeping their heads straight without running the risk of hurting them.

As will be seen from the following photographs the snaffle comes in many disguises. The bits have been grouped so that the reader can compare bits of the same type with each other – though some bits in each section will be considerably more severe than its neighbour. If one is not sure as to the severity or kindness of a bit then ask a reputable saddler, but the foregoing remarks should act as a guide and help the reader understand the many differences.

First we have the mullen-mouth snaffles, as in figs. 31, 32, 33, 34 and 35.
Eggbutt mullen in vulcanite (or rubber). Fig. 31.
Wire-ring mullen in vulcanite (or rubber). Fig. 32.
Eggbutt mullen mouth in metal. Fig. 33.
Wire-ring straight bar, in metal. Fig. 34.
Wire-ring straight bar stallion snaffle with twisted mouth. Fig. 35.

The many jointed snaffles come next. This is by far the largest group, and also the most varied, as is seen in figs. 36 to 71.

Though essentially a snaffle, I have separated the bridoon from its big brother, as they can only be used in conjunction with a curb bit. A normal bridoon will be seen under the double group, but figs. 72 to 79 are all variations.

More specialist than the other snaffles are those bits that form part of a bridle, i.e. they can only be used on a particular type of bridle head, and not on an ordinary one. Under this heading come figs. 80 to 84.

Other snaffles closely related to some of the former ones, and worthy of note, are described below. I have been unable to photograph them but do not wish to exclude them from my list.

Cable link – a rough link-chain snaffle.
Fillis* – similar to fig. 48, but with a hinged port in place of joint.
French Bridoon* – similar to Dr. Bristol but the plate lies flat.

Closely allied to the ordinary snaffle is the gag, whose name speaks for itself. It differs from the former in the fact that instead of the bridle head and reins being

* Can be seen in Captain Hartley Edwards *Saddlery*.

attached to the bit rings the bridle head passes through small holes in each ring (fig. 85), and thence, by way of the reins, to the rider's hands, enabling him to haul the bit high up in the horse's mouth. Its prime object is to raise the head and it acts on the corners of the mouth. Though a certain amount of pressure comes on to the poll, the upward force outweighs that of the lowering effect of the poll pressure. Gags are found with several mouthpieces besides a plain one; of these the twisted and roller mouthpieces, together with the double mouthpiece, are very severe. Sometimes a gag is used to replace the bridoon in a double, in which case they have smaller rings and thinner mouthpieces. On no account should these thin gags be used on their own, for as such they are nothing short of an invention of the devil. Any form of gag is only tolerable in the hands of an experienced horseman and should never be put into the hands of the inexperienced, or of a rough rider. See figs. 86 to 93. Col. Rodzianko, a roller gag, is not illustrated here.

The last snaffle group is that made up of the specialist and breaking bits. Of these, the best known are the breaking and mouthing bits with keys. Like other snaffles, they are found with straight and jointed mouthpieces and in several different materials. The specialist bits, on the other hand, cover both those bits that have been made to cure some habit or defect, and those, like the American check bits, which are snaffles, though at first glance they do not resemble one. These check bits are used principally on trotting horses, and are made in England for the American market. A few check bits, though, are used in this country as specialist bits for some reason or other. In general they do not come into the layman's sphere, for they are very much the experts' province and as such should be left alone.

Taking the breaking bits first, we have four to choose from: figs. 94 to 97.
Next we have the lead and stallion bits: figs. 98 to 103.
Specialist bits are those in figs. 104 to 105.
Though not illustrated, the following also come into this section:
Anti-lug* – resembles a Y-mouth, in so much that it has one pair of arms of uneven length (a Y-mouth, fig. 68 has two such arms).
Circle cheek* is similar to a metropolitan, but with a jointed mouth.
Flute or Windsuckers bit* is a straight hollow bar with wire rings and holes in the mouthpiece to allow air to pass through it.

We now come to the American bits, starting with a bit which owing to its make-up I have removed from the general list. It is not a bit for the ordinary horseman. Figs. 106 to 113.

This concludes the snaffle group in all its many variations and disguises, though in fact there are some others, but they are no longer important.

The double bridle group follows the snaffle in importance, for once a horse's training has reached a sufficient standard he must be introduced to a combination of a curb and bridoon, as the snaffle is now called, if his education is to pass beyond the elementary stage and reach the greater heights that are there for the schooling. This group is now smaller than it used to be, many of the curbs having fallen into disuse. The two bits

* Can be seen in Captain Hartley Edwards Saddlery.

take their names from the French, bride, to bridle and oon, to borrow, and the Latin, *curvus*, to bend. The bridoon can be spelt bradoon, either is correct, but the British Horse Society and the Pony Club favour the former.

Of the curb bits, the best known are the Weymouth with or without a port or tongue groove, i.e. a mullen or ported mouth, the latter being known sometimes as a Cambridge mouth, and the Banbury. The Weymouth can have either a long or short cheek, and a fixed or sliding mouthpiece. In the latter the cheek passes through the mouthpiece allowing a certain freedom of movement up and down, whereas with the Banbury the mouthpiece passes through the cheek allowing the two cheeks to rotate independently of each other (fig. 114). By this means pressure can be brought to bear on one side of the mouth alone, whereas with the Weymouth the two cheeks work in conjunction with one another. Unlike the Weymouth there is no port as such, but the straight mouthpiece can have an ''hour-glass'' middle. This is necessary as the mouth-piece, too, rotates and the horse can roll it round in his mouth if he should wish to do so. A port, or tongue groove (a very low port), however low, would prevent this.

With a double, one pair of reins are carried by the bridoon and another by the curb, enabling the rider to use each bit individually. In the case of the bridoon it is usual to have loose wire rings, but both eggbutt and gags are quite common. As with all curbs, the severity of the action is judged by the length of the cheeks above and below the mouthpiece. The longer the cheek the greater the leverage, and therefore the sharper the action. A very short cheeked or ''Tom-Thumb'' curb is the gentlest of the Weymouths and in itself a kind bit which can cause little or no harm once the horse has learnt to accept and understand it. In the case of the fixed mouthpiece the action is more direct, but the leverage less. The object of the curb, used in conjunction with a bridoon, is to maintain the head carriage and induce flexion, once the head has been placed at the correct height by the bridoon (fig. 115). This is achieved by applying pressure to the tongue, bars, curb-groove, by means of the curb chain, which acts as a fulcrum and without which a curb would just be another snaffle, and the poll. If a high port is employed, then the roof of the mouth also comes into play. By obtaining true flexion we gain direct contact with our horse and are able to convey to him our wishes without fuss or bother, but care must be taken not to lose the balance between the curb and bridoon. Too much curb, unsupported by the bridoon will cause the horse to overbend (fig. 116), which is a fault. The two bits must balance each other. In the old days many more types of curbs were employed, but on the whole these have gone out of fashion, so, too, to a large extent has the rough-sided mouthpiece, which, a few years back, was found on most Weymouth bits. The idea was that either side could be used and the effect was similar to that of a twisted snaffle. Nowadays, many more bits are made plain on both sides, which is an excellent thing. If a rough-sided bit should be in use, then the smooth side should be next to the lips, i.e. inwards.

Starting with the more usual bits from this group, we pass to those bits which are essentially curbs, and the American counterparts of our bits, the walking horse and racking bits. *See* figs. 117 to 135.

The Pelham group, deriving its name from the Pelham family, is a large one and consists not only of those bits using two reins, i.e. a true Pelham, but also those using only one. In this group I have included those driving bits (other than those coming under the snaffle group), which are by nature Pelhams, for sometimes these find their way on to and into the unfortunate mouths of show-jumpers!

The Pelham is the grafting together of one or more features from the snaffle and curb groups to produce a single mouthpiece with a combined action of the two bits. In most cases two reins are used, but one rein is adopted in some circumstances. In short, a Pelham is a curb with a built-in snaffle. Most features found in each group will be found in the Pelham, i.e. fixed or sliding mouthpieces – ported or mullen – jointed or eggbutt – Banbury and so on, giving a vast variety of similar, but slightly different bits. Like the snaffle, rubber, vulcanite and metal are used for the mouthpieces, and so, too, are rollers. The principle of a single bit is sound enough, but in theory it is impossible to use both reins at once and get a definite action from either (fig. 136). For this reason it is not a sensible bit. Nevertheless, as I said in the introduction to the art of bitting, Pelhams for all their faults suit some horses, owing to their conformation, but in general it is better to try either a snaffle or double bridle before resorting to a Pelham. In the case of a young horse graduating from a snaffle, then it is only wise to use a double, for a Pelham can only cause confusion and may well result in a faulty head carriage. For instead of flexing correctly from the poll (fig. 115), with a nice arch to his neck (but not in the middle of his neck) he will tend to set his neck against the Pelham, shortening up the muscles along his crest and lengthening those underneath his neck along his windpipe, until he becomes almost ewe-necked (fig. 136). This is completely wrong and must be avoided at all costs. It is often seen in children's ponies and some-times hacks, both of which get introduced to a Pelham too early in their education in the mistaken idea that it is a short cut to the show-ring and a stepping stone to a double. Instead it is just a passport to a faulty head carriage that is extremely hard to correct, though with hours of hard strapping to tone up the muscles along the crest, coupled with careful riding in one of the former bits, it can be done. Even so, if a horse has been ridden too young in a Pelham instead of a snaffle, it will be hard to return to a plain snaffle, for the mouth will have suffered and the horse versed in such delightful tricks as getting the bit between its teeth!

See figs. 137 to 161.

Besides these bits, the following, though now out of date to a large extent, are worthy of a mention.

Thurlow, instead of having the usual round eye at the top of the cheek to take the bridle head, has an elongated one shaped like a bird's beak, pointing to the rear.

Egglink Pelham has a mouthpiece similar to a Dick Christian snaffle.

Harry Highover's is a curb with the bridoon mouthpieces jointed on to each side to the port of the curb; outwardly it would look like a double.

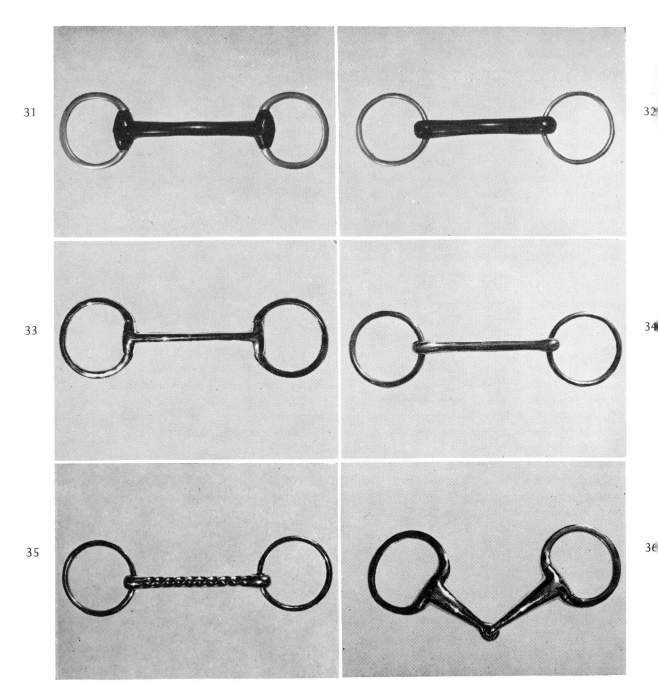

31

32

33

34

35

36

Fig. 31. Eggbutt mullen snaffle (vulcanite). Fig. 32. Wire-ring vulcanite mullen snaffle.
Fig. 33. Eggbutt mullen mouth snaffle in metal. Fig. 34. Wire-ring straight bar snaffle.
Fig. 35. Wire-ring straight bar stallion snaffle Fig. 36. German eggbutt snaffle. Jointed.
    with twisted mouth.

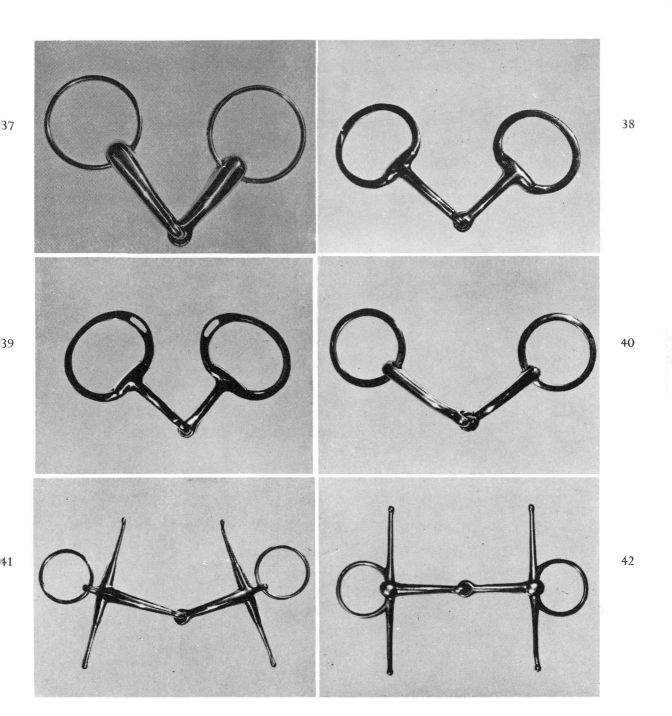

Fig. 37. Wire-ring German snaffle. Jointed (21).

Fig. 38. Jointed eggbutt snaffle.

Fig. 39. Jointed slotted eggbutt snaffle.

Fig. 40. Flat-ring jointed snaffle. Irish snaffle.

Fig. 41. Australian loose-ring or Fulmer snaffle.

Fig. 42. Ball-cheek snaffle.

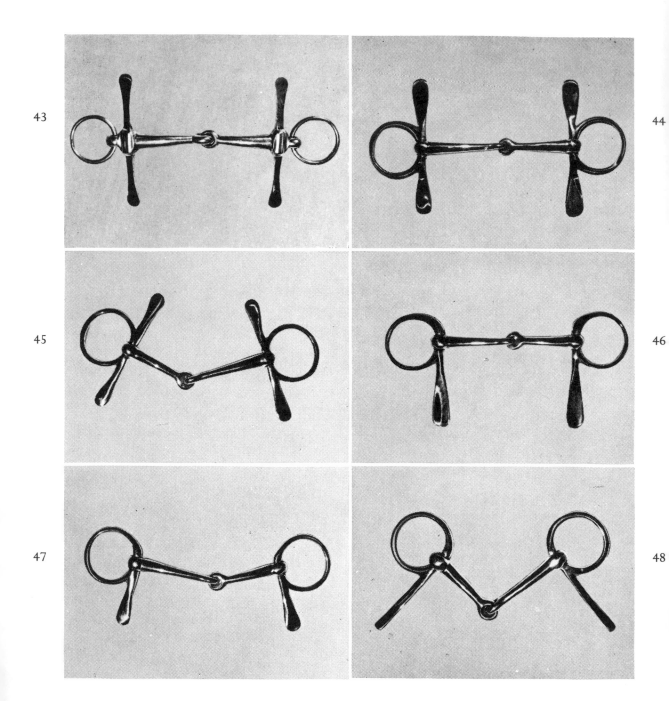

Fig. 43. Loose-ring spoon-cheek snaffle.
Fig. 45. New Zealand full spoon-cheek snaffle.
Fig. 47. New Zealand half spoon-cheek snaffle.

Fig. 44. Full spoon-cheek snaffle.
Fig. 46. Half spoon-cheek snaffle.
Fig. 48. Late eighteenth-century type half spoon
snaffle. Forerunner of the ostrich.

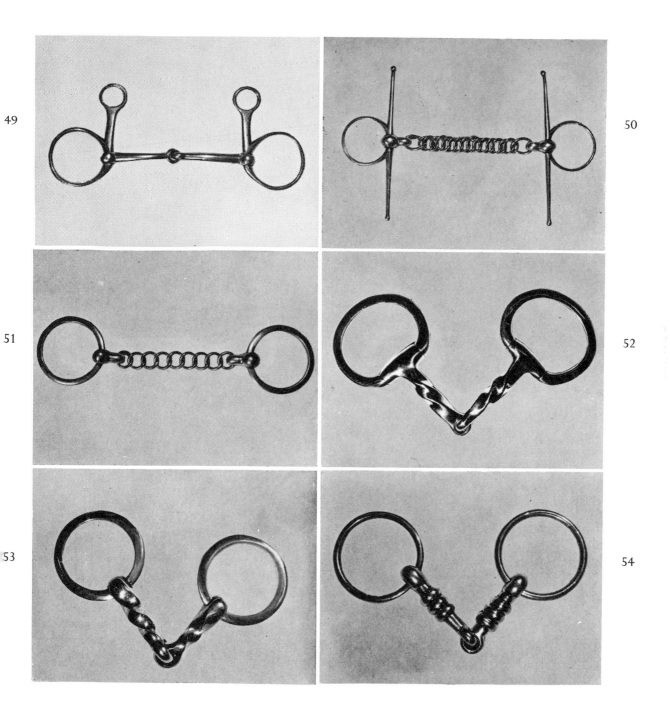

Fig. 49. Hanging-cheek snaffle.

Fig. 51. Single-link chain mouth, flat-ring snaffle.

Fig. 53. Flat-ring twisted-jointed snaffle.

Fig. 50. Double-link chain mouth, cheek snaffle.

Fig. 52. Twisted-jointed eggbutt snaffle.

Fig. 54. Wire-ring jointed snaffle with rollers round the mouth.

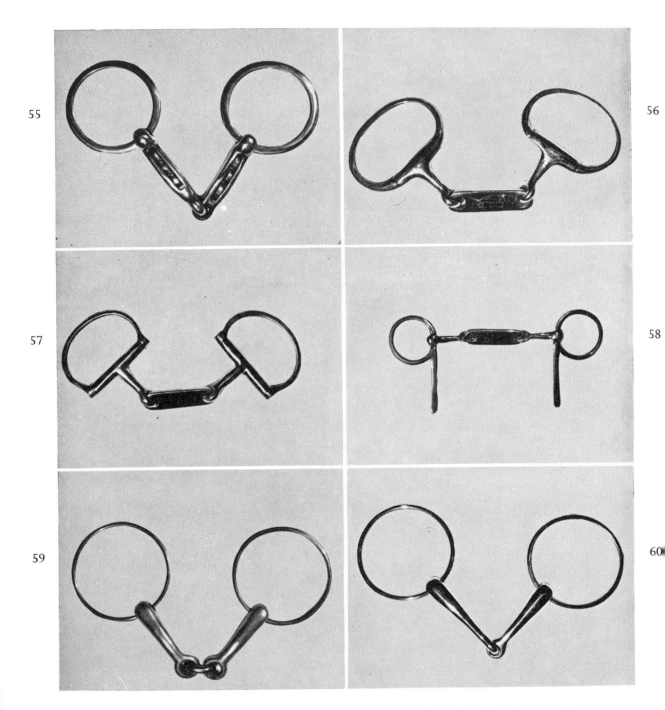

Fig. 55. Magenis snaffle.
Fig. 57. Dee-cheek Dr. Bristol race snaffle.
Fig. 59. Dick Christian snaffle.

Fig. 56. Eggbutt Dr. Bristol race snaffle.
Fig. 58. Dr. Bristol half spoon-cheek snaffle.
Fig. 60. Wire-ring tapered race snaffle.

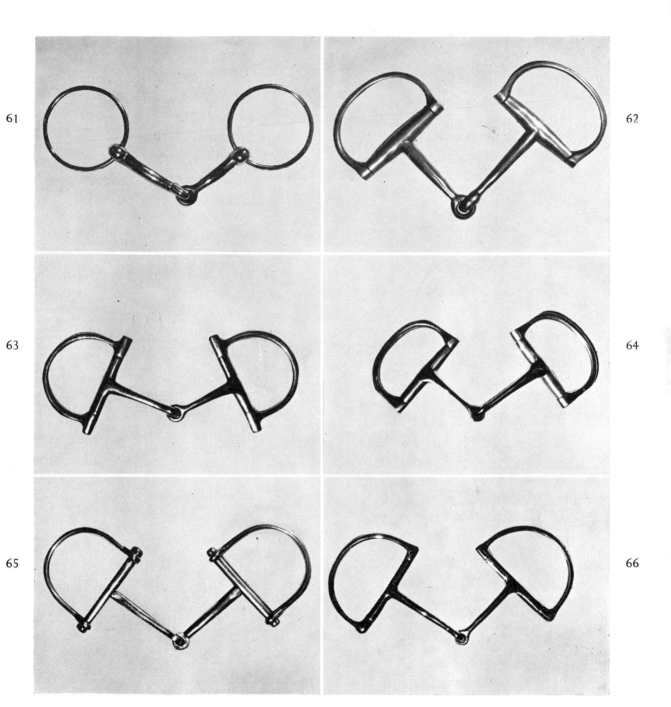

Fig. 61. Wire-ring race snaffle.
Fig. 63. American Dee-cheek race snaffle.
Fig. 65. Dee-cheek snaffle.

Fig. 62. Dee-cheek race snaffle.
Fig. 64. Dee-cheek – alum-steel race snaffle.
Fig. 66. Myers Dee-cheek snaffle (22).

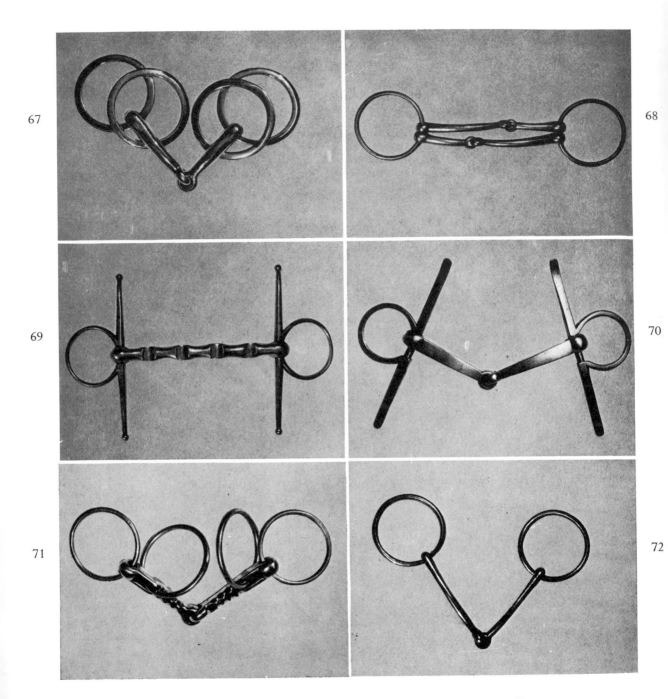

67

68

69

70

71

72

Fig. 67. Flat-ring Wilson snaffle.
Fig. 69. Wellington snaffle.
Fig. 71. Scorrier or Cornish snaffle.

Fig. 68. Y or W mouth snaffle.
Fig. 70. Square mouth cheek snaffle.
Fig. 72. Extra-thin jointed bridoon (23).

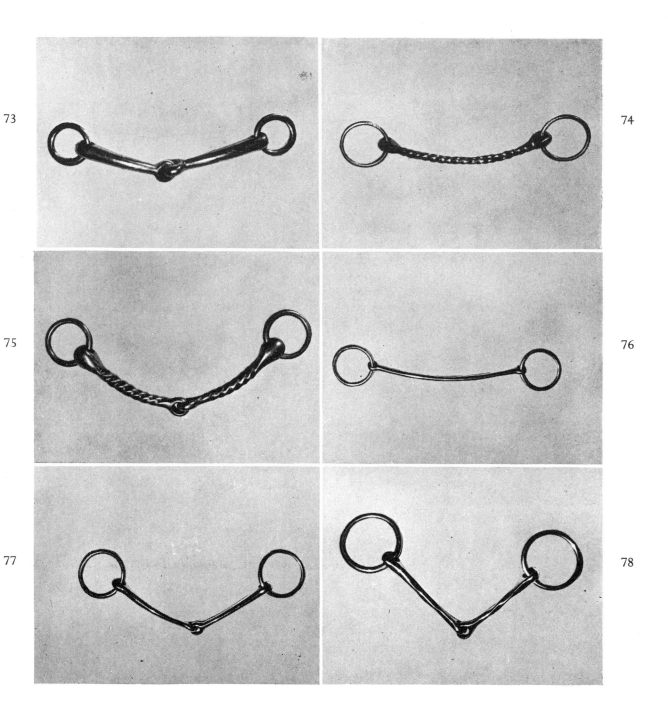

Fig. 73. Jointed-check bridoon.
Fig. 75. Wire ring twisted-jointed check bri-
    doon.
Fig. 77. American jointed check.

Fig. 74. Wire-ring twisted-mullen check bri-
    doon.
Fig. 76. American mullen-mouth check.
Fig. 78. American twisted-jointed check.

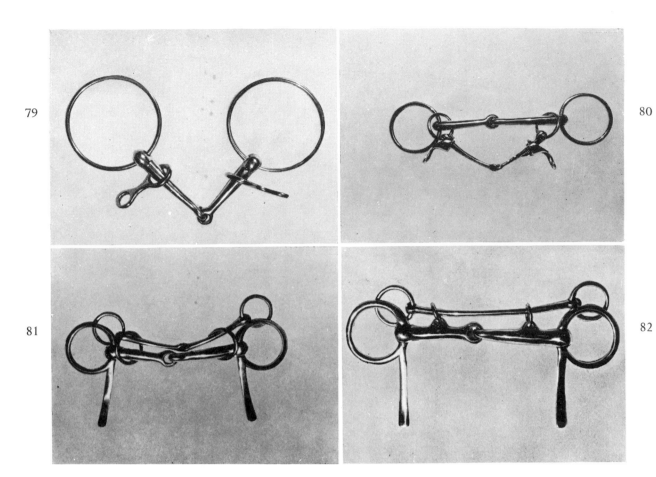

79
80
81
82

Fig. 79. Rockwell snaffle (28).
Fig. 81. Six-ring race snaffle, form of Citation.

Fig. 80. Norton Perfection snaffle (27). Improved pattern.
Fig. 82. Norton Perfection or Citation.

85
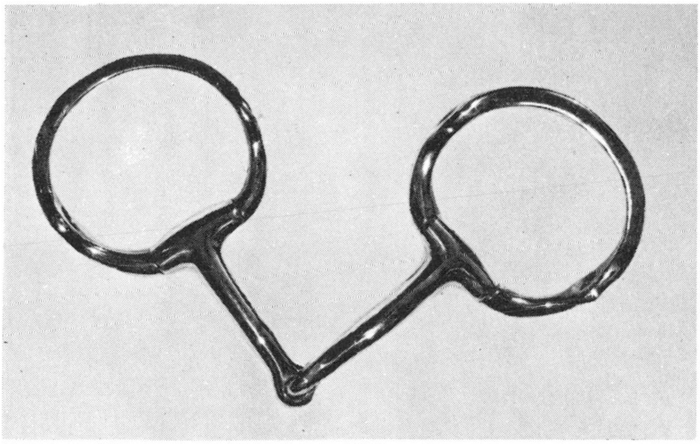

86
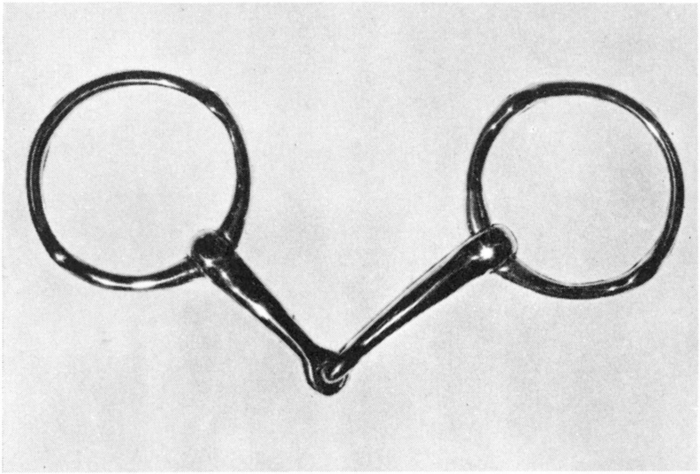

87
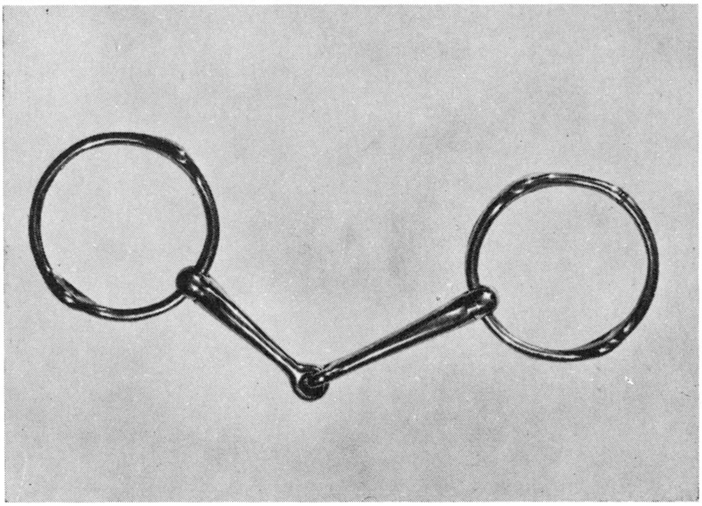

83
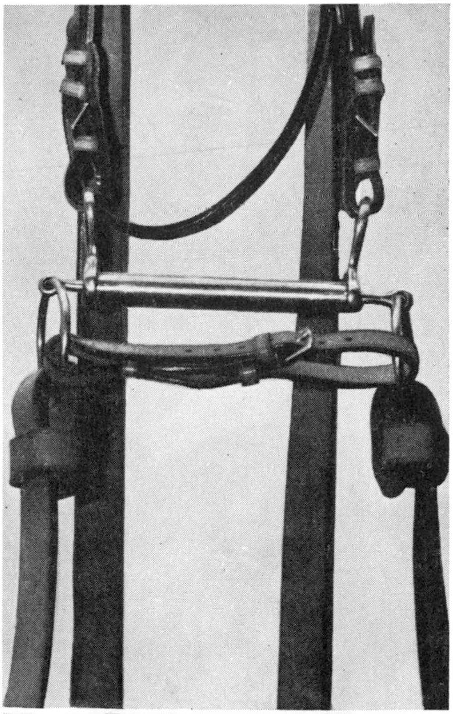

84
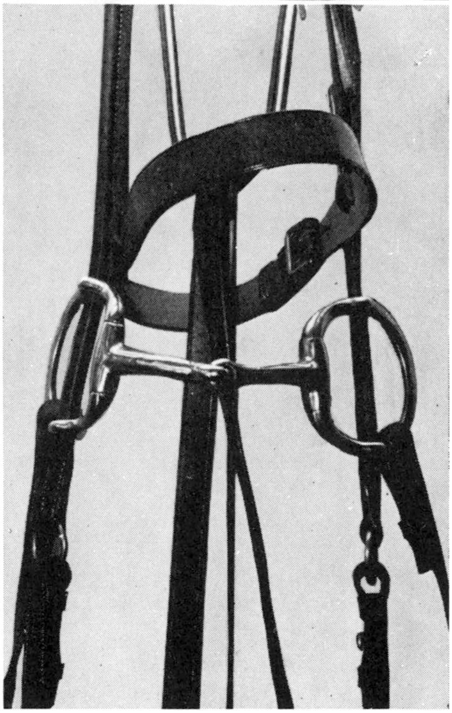

Fig. 85. Cheltenham gag.
Fig. 86. Balding gag.
Fig. 87. Salisbury gag.

Fig. 83. American revolving slide-mouth snaffle.
Fig. 84. Gag showing bridle cheek passing through bit.

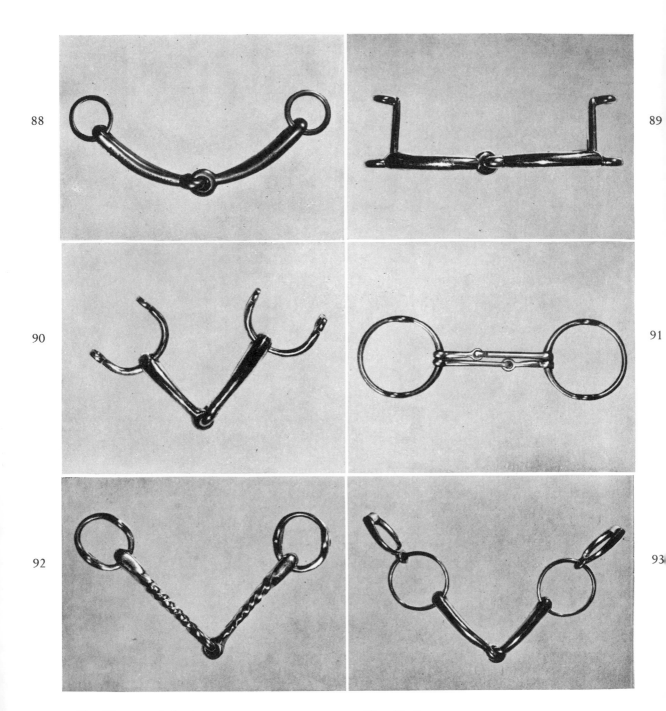

Fig. 88. Jointed-check gag.
Fig. 89. Duncan gag.
Fig. 90. Cecil Smith gag.
Fig. 91. Y or W mouth gag.
Fig. 92. Hack overcheck, cord type.
Fig. 93. Hitchcock gag, part of.

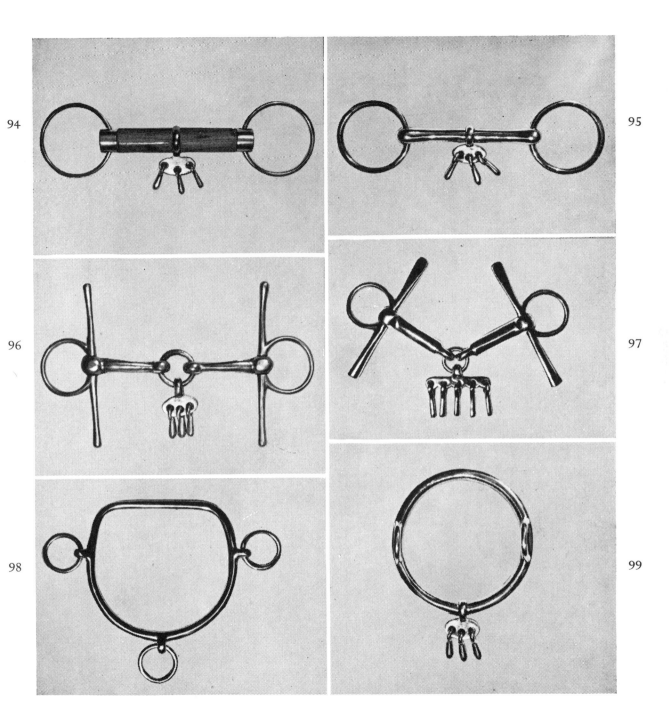

Fig. 94. Wire-ring wooden-mouth breaking bit with keys.
Fig. 96. Ball-cheek breaking bit with keys.
Fig. 98. Colt lead bit, Chifney.

Fig. 95. Bar-mouth breaking bit with keys.
Fig. 97. Heavy breaking bit with keys.
Fig. 99. Tattersall ring bit with keys.

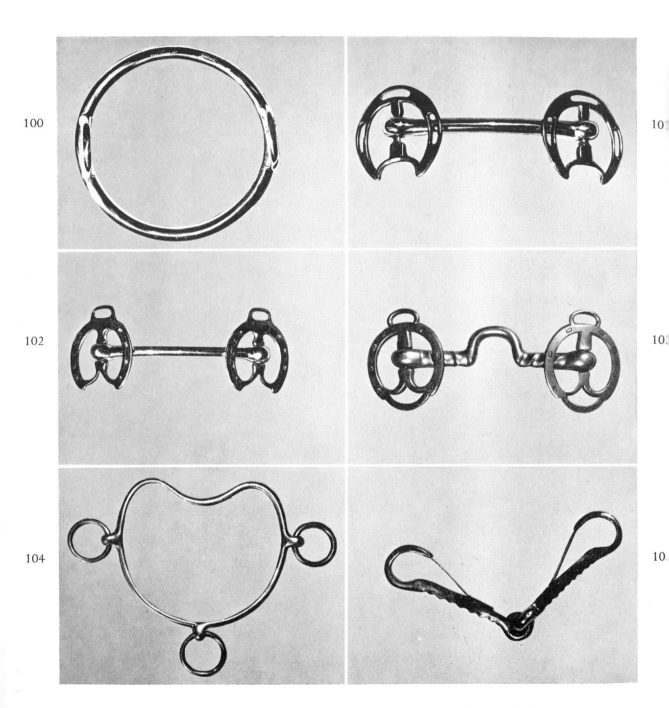

Fig. 100. Tattersall ring bit.
Fig. 102. Horseshoe-check mullen stallion
        show bit.
Fig. 104. Chifney anti-rear bit.

Fig. 101. Metropolitan stallion bit.
Fig. 103. Horseshoe-cheek bit with port.
Fig. 105. Spring-mouth or butterfly snaffle.

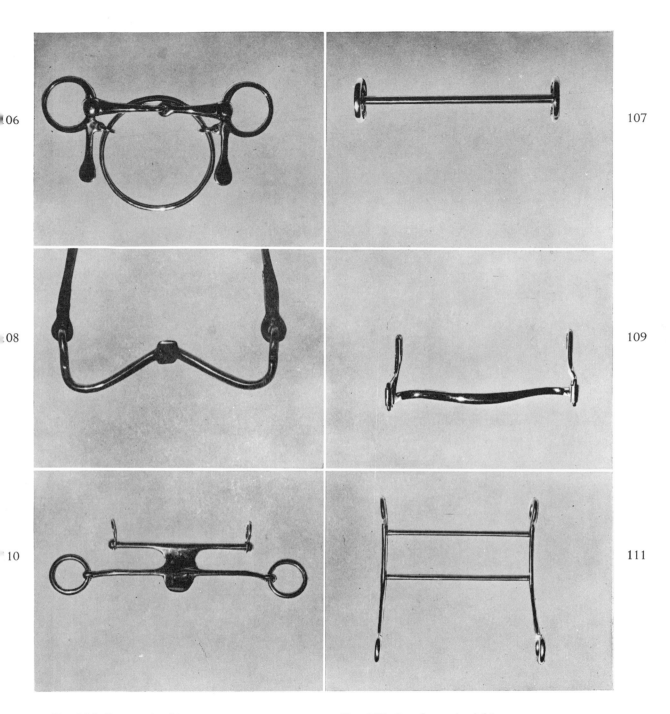

Fig. 106. Dexter ring bit.
Fig. 108. Burch check, tongue grid.
Fig. 110. McKerron check bit.
Fig. 107. Speedway-cheek bit.
Fig. 109. Hutton check bit.
Fig. 111. Crab check bit.

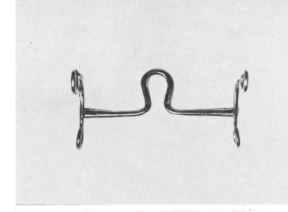
112

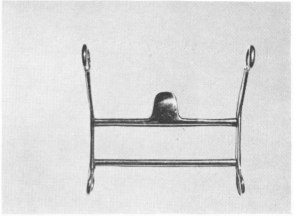
113

Fig. 112. Critt Davis check bit.
Fig. 113. Crab check with spoon.

115

Fig. 115. Using a curb in conjunction with a bridoon.

Fig. 116. Too much curb unsupported by bridoon.

11

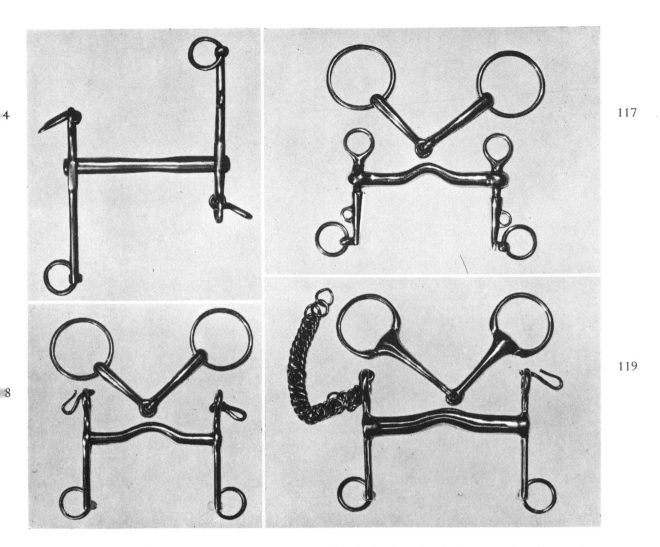

Fig. 114. Banbury-showing moving arms.
Fig. 118. Fixed-cheek Weymouth and bridoon.

Fig. 117. Short-cheek slide-mouth Weymouth and bridoon.
Fig. 119. Dressage Weymouth and eggbutt bridoon.

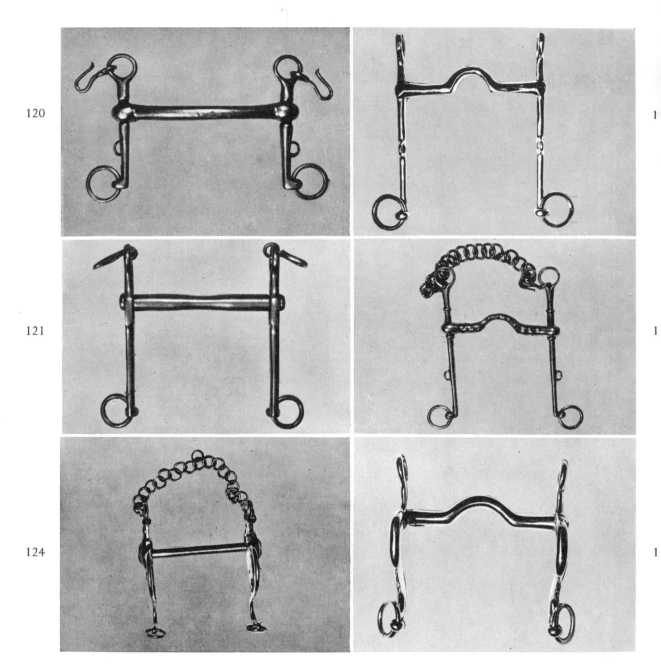

120

121

124

Fig. 120. Mullen slide-mouth Weymouth.
Fig. 121. Banbury.
Fig. 124. Military Banbury.

Fig. 122. Portsmouth show bit.
Fig. 123. Long-cheek Weymouth.
Fig. 125. Swan-cheek hack bit.

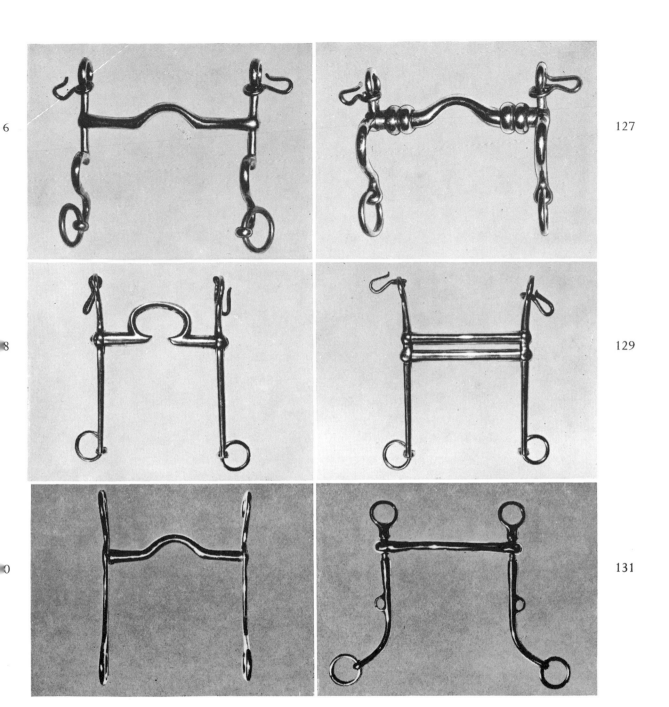

Fig. 126. Swan-cheek show Weymouth.
Fig. 128. Segundo bit.
Fig. 130. American Western Weymouth.

Fig. 127. Swan fixed-cheek roller hack.
Fig. 129. Double mouth bit, relative a Peter-
boro'.
Fig. 131. American slide mullen-mouth walking horse bit.

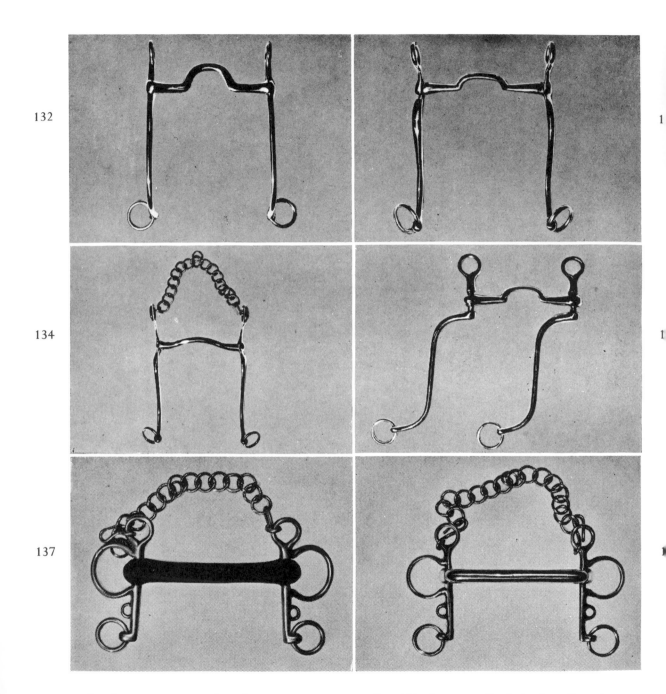

Fig. 132. American Racking bit.
Fig. 134. American heavy walking horse bit.
Fig. 137. Rubber mullen-mouth Pelham.

Fig. 133. American fixed-cheek walking horse bit.
Fig. 135. American turn-cheek walking horse bit.
Fig. 138. Scamperdale Pelham.

Fig. 136. No definite action from either.

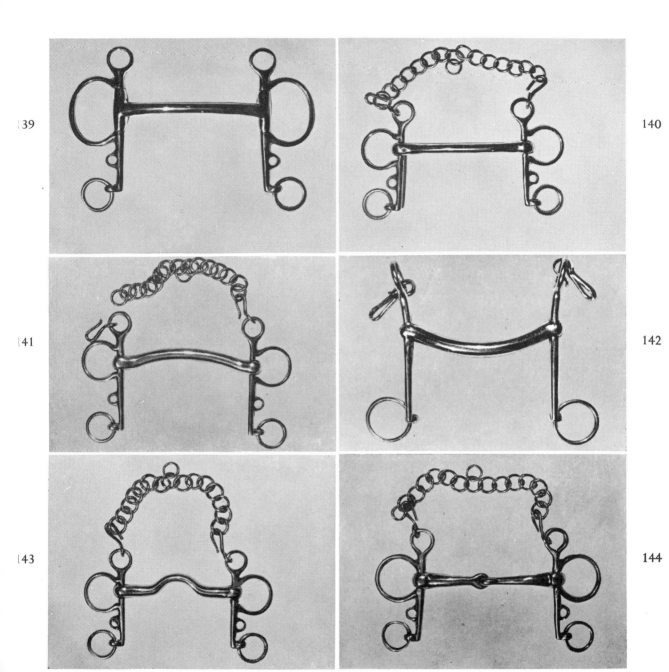

Fig. 139. Eggbutt mullen-mouth Pelham.
Fig. 141. Arch-mouth Pelham.
Fig. 143. Hartwell Pelham.

Fig. 140. Mullen-mouth Pelham.
Fig. 142. Reversed-arch Pelham.
Fig. 144. Jointed Pelham.

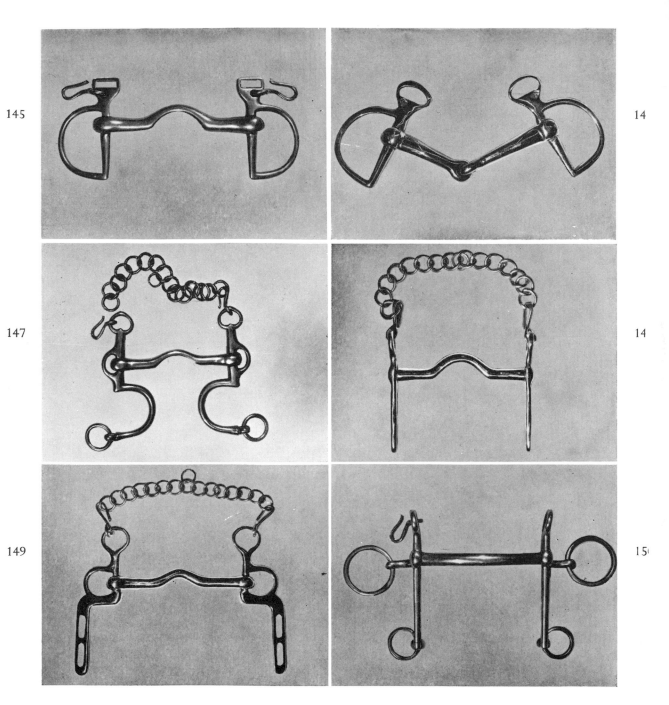

145

14

147

14

149

15

Fig. 145. Kimblewick, Cambridge-mouth; true Kimblewick.

Fig. 146. Kimblewick, jointed mouth.

Fig. 147. Show hack Cambridge mouth Pelham.

Fig. 148. Ninth Lancer.

Fig. 149. Reversible army or angle-cheek Pelham.

Fig. 150. Rugby Pelham.

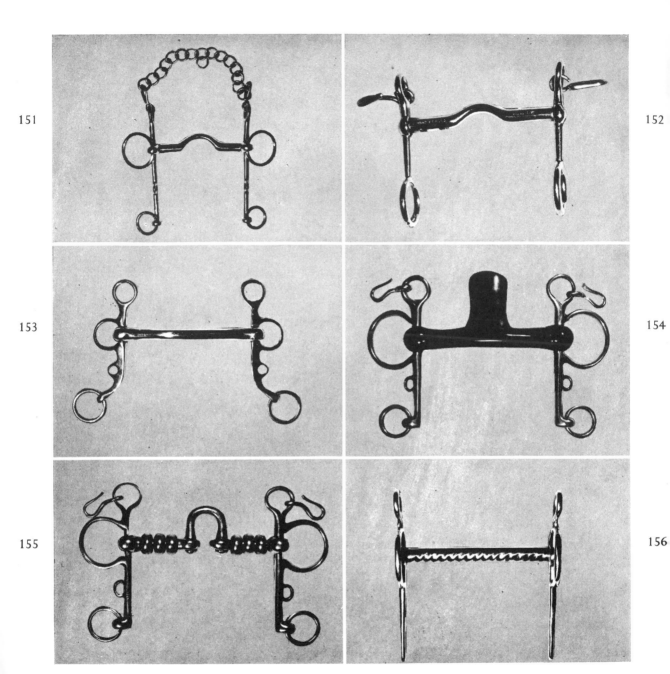

Fig. 151. Loose-ring Pelham.

Fig. 152. Globe-cheek Pelham.

Fig. 153. American Pelham. This was formerly very much an English bit.

Fig. 154. Port-mouth tongue Pelham.

Fig. 155. Hanoverian Pelham.

Fig. 156. Fixed-cheek Liverpool.

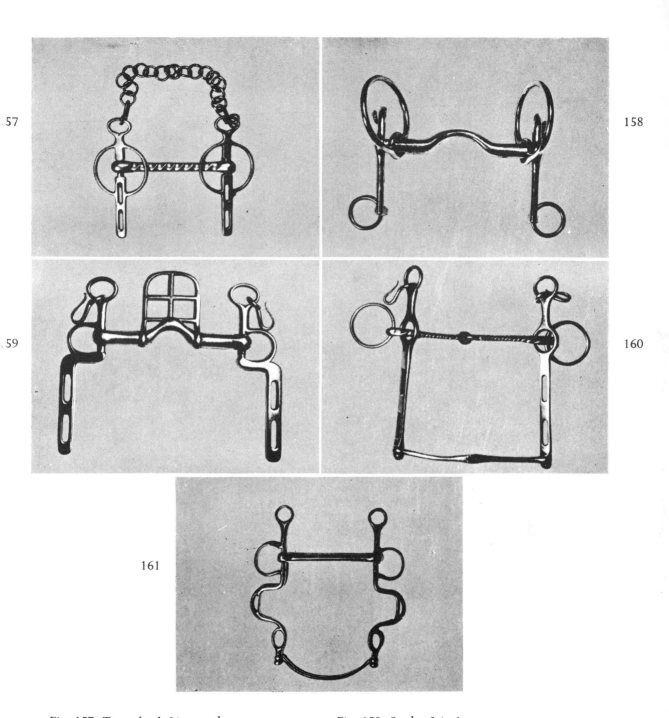

Fig. 157. Turn-cheek Liverpool.
Fig. 158. Swales 3-in-1.
Fig. 159. Angle-cheek Pelham with grid.
Fig. 160. Stockton, not standard pattern.
Fig. 161. Buxton coaching bit.

CHAPTER FOUR

CURB CHAINS

No curb bit is complete without a curb chain of some kind. I am including the five most common ones. Like bits, they can be made in more than one material. In this case, metal, elastic and leather, with rubber used as a guard, form the basic choices. The principle of these being metal, from which the single and double link chains are made. The single link (fig. 162) is the best known, but is most likely to rub and pinch and to be probably the severer of the two. Personally, I prefer and use the double link (fig. 163), as it has a smoother surface. Next comes the leather curb chain (fig. 164), sometimes known as a humane curb chain. This has the centre part made of leather with links at each end. Providing it is kept clean, it is an excellent one, being much kinder and less likely to pinch or rub than the chain ones. It is very useful on a horse that dislikes a metal chain, or one that hardly needs a chain at all, having a sensitive mouth. For the horse that resents having its jaw held in an unyielding grip, the elastic curb chain is the answer (fig. 165); this allows a certain amount of give and some horses appreciate this. Lastly, we have a severe curb chain that owes its origin and name to India. The Jodhphor polo curb chain (fig. 166), unlike the others, has a large oval link in the centre which can exert a fair degree of pressure. The link is covered in leather, though I believe some forms are plain. To fit these chains, stand on the near side and wind them clockwise till the links lie flat. The width of the chains also vary, and like the bits, the thicker and wider the chain the kinder the action.

In the event of a metal chain rubbing, then a rubber guard will help prevent this and ensure some measure of relief to the horse. But whatever type of chain is used it is essential to remove the long hairs from the back of the chin and out of the chin groove. These only catch in the curb chain (or any strap that passes through the groove), and causes great discomfort, even to the extent of raw bleeding. So be sure to see that all excess hair has been removed to avoid trouble and let air circulate freely round the area, for it is one of the places where a horse sweats most. When unsaddling and bridling after a ride it is a good thing to either let the horse dowse his face, minus the bridle, in the water trough, or else to sponge the curb groove and lips to remove any sweat and saliva before it has chance to dry on. For if left, it is one of the prime causes of bitting galls and sores.

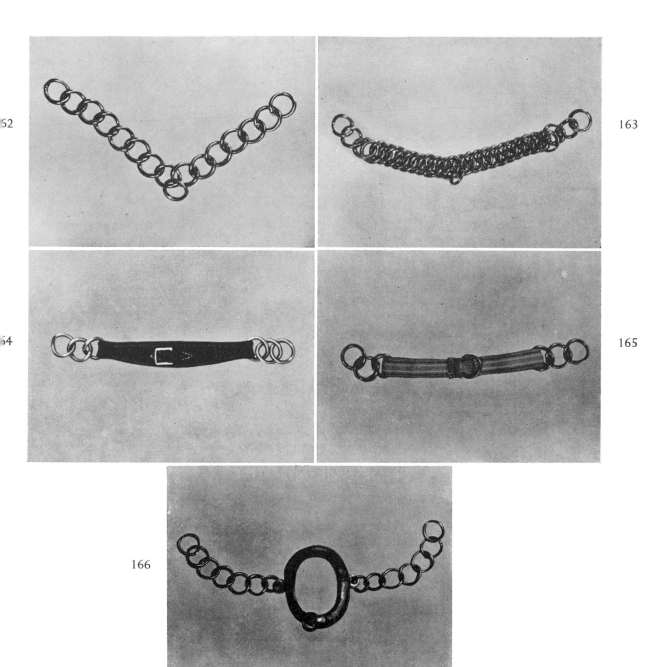

Fig. 162. Single-link curb chain   Fig. 163. Double-link curb chain.
Fig. 164. Leather curb chain.   Fig. 165. Elastic curb chain.
Fig. 166. Jodhphor polo curb chain.

CHAPTER FIVE

AN OUTWARD GLANCE —
SOME BETTER-KNOWN BITS AND THEIR FITTING

IT is one thing to look at a vast number of bits on their own. It is not so easy to picture these same bits on a horse. For this reason I have picked out a few of the better-known bits, together with one or two of their lesser-known brethren, so that we can take a closer look at them and their fitting.

From the snaffle group I have taken three of the more popular members; the others follow, in some degree or other, the same theme and therefore conform to the general rule.

The fitting of a snaffle is important. It must neither be too high, nor too low in the mouth, but fit snugly into the corners without wrinkling them. If fitted too low it will only catch against the front teeth and encourage the horse to put his tongue over the bit. A habit once formed that is hard to cure. On the other hand, if too high the horse will have its lips stretched and eventually they will become sore and cracked, causing pain and discomfort. Both will lead to an unpleasant ride, for which the rider alone will be to blame. Care, too, must be exercised in seeing that the bit is the right width for the mouth – too wide it will only move from side to side and cause bruising of the lips – too narrow and it will pinch, causing equal pain and discomfort. To measure a snaffle bit, lay it flat on a table or similar surface and take the measurement from the inside of one ring to the inside of the other. A quarter of an inch can make all the difference between a bit that fits and one that is too big or too small. In general, a mullen-mouth will be a bit smaller than a jointed bit, the reason being one lies flat all the time, the other loses some of its width through its joint. A saddler will tell you the size you need; it is impossible to lay down a hard and fast rule, some ponies have big heads and will take a bit intended for a hunter or cob, while a hunter, if clean bred, will take a bit catalogued for a cob or pony. The only sane answer is to measure the width of the mouth, inside, from lip to lip, before buying a new bit. In this way a good fit is assured.

Nowadays, one frequently sees a snaffle accompanied by some form of drop noseband. A well-schooled horse with a light mouth and no bit evasion tricks should go quietly and sensibly in a plain snaffle without any outside aid from a noseband. All the same, for schooling, and on some horses, a drop noseband is a great asset if correctly fitted and not abused. There are several patterns and I have illustrated but two. Though not seen very frequently, the adjustable drop noseband (fig. 167) has its advantages. No two horses' heads are the same width, and to fit correctly, the front of the band must reach the right spot, i.e. in line with the prominent cheek bone and lie two and a half to three inches above the nostrils, otherwise it is not possible to pass the strap correctly below the bit before fastening it in the curb groove, where it should lie snugly and not too tightly. Two fingers must be able to be slipped under the front of the nose-band or, alternatively, under the back strap in the curb groove, otherwise the noseband is too tight and the horse will slowly boil up and lose his temper – and who can blame him – not his rider!

In fig. 167 Castania is wearing her everyday bridle, an eggbutt-sided, plain-jointed snaffle, in conjunction with an adjustable-drop noseband. Owing to her habit (learnt when she was being broken) of grabbing her bit in her teeth it is not now possible, except on special occasions, to ride her in a snaffle without a drop noseband. This is quite a common bit evasion, and an extremely tiresome one, for it does not mean necessarily that the horse has a hard mouth, but on the contrary it often denotes a soft mouth. The habit, for I do not regard this as a vice, starts with the horse feeling pain from its bit, catching hold of it to avoid hurting its mouth; having discovered this is possible they then use the same trick to obtain their own wish and have a good gallop whenever they think it would be fun. It is in cases like this that the drop noseband, not too tight, is a great blessing, for it gives us the control we need without resorting to the use of a stronger bit. Of all the snaffles, this bit is the most widely used and probably deservedly so. For an all-round bit, it is hard to beat. Not only is it kind, but the eggbutt sides, as I explained earlier, prevent the risk of rubbing or chaffing. Provided a horse has a snaffle mouth this is about the best bit for a novice to choose, for most horses, with few exceptions will go kindly in it.

Closely allied to the eggbutt, but with the added advantage of a loose ring, giving a greater degree of play in the horse's mouth to help it mouth, comes the Australian loose ring, or as we know it in this country, Fulmer snaffle. It was the Halls of the famous Fulmer riding establishment who made the bit so popular, hence its name. They have used it widely for a long time. Unlike the eggbutt, this bit has long cheeks and can be used in its natural state, as in fig. 168, when it is just like any other jointed snaffle, or, as shown in fig. 169, complete with keepers and an ordinary drop noseband. This is its most common guise. Now compare the two photographs (figs. 168 and 169). In the first, Castania is wearing it normally. The bridle head is in direct line with the end of the bit, letting the bit act principally on the tongue and corners of the mouth, with the sides of the bars a poor third; whereas in the second photograph, Shelton's bridle head is at about forty-five degrees to the cheek of the bit, where it is fixed by a keeper. This means that the bit now comes into action, not only on the tongue and slightly at the corners of the mouth, but much more on the bars and sides of the bars which now become the principle point of contact. This gives a greater degree of control, and when used with a drop noseband, which uses both the nose and curb groove as points of control as well, a creditable amount of flexion can be obtained.

For a horse with a dry mouth, a fixed-mouth bit is not a sensible one, and a greater degree of mouthing will be obtained from a loose-ringed bit. For this reason, if a cheeked bit is used, a loose-ring spoon-cheeked bit might be quite a reasonable choice (fig. 42), for with the flatter cheeks the bit is less likely to get caught up in something it has no business to be caught in. On the other hand, if a cheeked bit is not necessary, then a wire-ring German snaffle is an excellent bit (fig. 37).

For my final bit from this group, I have taken one from the other end of the scale: a Scorrier or Cornish snaffle (fig. 170). This is as harsh and severe as the other two are kind and gentle. (I have not included figs. 42 and 37; they, too, are kind bits.) Unlike normal bits, it has a square-jointed mouthpiece, one side of which is plain and the other twisted or serrated (fig. 71). Built on the Wilson principle, it has four rings, the inner two carrying the bridle head run in slots in the mouthpiece; this tends to make the bit reverse itself in the mouth, i.e. the joint instead of pointing towards the front of the mouth points towards the back of the throat, causing, I feel sure, a certain amount of annoyance, to say the least of it. The other two rings carry the reins alone, and through the influence of the inner rings sliding towards the centre of the bit when pressure is applied to the reins, a squeezing effect is produced on the outer jaw-bones and cheeks, lips, etc., as well as the usual snaffle-bit action. This, coupled with the twisted, square mouth, makes the bit extremely sharp. It is a bit I have little time for, as it can cut the corners of the mouth to ribbons and cause a great deal of damage, especially if the slots are allowed to become rough-edged. The square mouth, too, tends to dig into the bars of the mouth and cause lasting harm. I have shown it for one reason only, its growing popularity. I believe few riders quite realize what they are inflicting on their unfortunate horses when they choose this bit. In experienced hands it might have its advantages on an extremely hard mouth that is beyond redemption, but the expert horseman is a law unto himself and few and far between. For the average rider it is a dangerous bit, as it inflicts far too much pain. This is very cruel and only makes matters worse in the long run. If one has ever seen a mouth after being cut by this bit, I am sure no rider would knowingly choose it again. Incidentally, it was the only bit Castania tossed her head with and fussed over, hence the reason I can be seen standing at her shoulder! (fig. 170).

Passing to the second group, we now come to the doubles. The fitting principles for a snaffle apply to all bridles, and the double is no exception. Like its big brother, the bridoon should fit snugly into the corners of the mouth, with the curb directly below it, care being taken to see that both bits fit easily (fig. 171). Having fitted the two bits, the curb chain, fixed to a curb hook on the off side (it is suspended from the eye of the curb bit that takes the bridle head), is then, with the rider standing on the near side, wound in a clockwise direction (to the right) until the links lie flat. Once this has been achieved the chain passes under the bridoon (like the back strap of the drop noseband with a snaffle) and is linked on to the near side curb hook by slipping the bottom of the required link on to the hook. In this way the chain will remain flat and if properly adjusted, will come into action when the cheeks of the curb bit are drawn back to an angle of 45 degrees. The lip strap, which is fastened to the small dees on the lower arms of the curb cheeks, is then passed through the single link at the bottom centre of the curb chain and fastened loosely. The object of the lip strap is to prevent loss of the chain should it come unhooked, and to keep the cheeks of a Banbury bit from revolving forward and up beyond a certain degree. It also helps to stop a horse from catching the cheeks in his teeth.

The most popular of the doubles is probably the short-cheeked, slide-mouth Weymouth, with a wire-ring bridoon (fig. 172). It is a simple double and, correctly adjusted, a well-trained horse should go well in it. Castania has always been shown and hunted in one, and also uses it very often for hunter trials and one-day events, besides show-jumping when she is not wearing a snaffle. She is a strong pony who likes to go on, but has, even at 16, a fairly sensitive mouth which is not strictly a hard mouth, for this reason she likes two bits. She can play with them, and if the rider does not hang on her mouth she will respect the bits; but should she find her mouth being pulled at she in her turn will pull back. For this reason, like all horses, it behoves the rider to treat her mouth with respect.

In recent years, with the growing popularity of dressage, the fixed-cheek Weymouth (fig. 173) has become more in vogue, and was for a while obligatory in all advanced dressage tests.

For my last double I have taken the dressage Weymouth with its German mouth-pieces and eggbutt bridoon (fig. 174). With both bits fixed the action is more positive than with the slide-mouth and loose-ring combination, and the horse cannot "play" with them so easily, thereby keeping its mind more on the job in hand. I was very interested in how well Castania went in this bridle for it was the first time she had worn it. She accepted the bits willingly, taking an instant liking to their thickness and mouthing freely. It was also the first time I had ridden with these bits, and I was delighted with the way I was able to obtain a true head carriage without difficulty (fig. 175), and in the shortest space of time, using only very light aids. For it must be remembered that I only arrived the night before. Castania had been enjoying her summer's rest at grass, coming up, still unshod, to take part in these photographs, so neither of us had had time to grow accustomed to these bits. We merely resumed our old partnership, a partnership that, regardless of the years between, has never been broken. Incidentally, for none of these photographs did I carry or use either stick or spur, but relied entirely on natural aids to obtain the results I required. For all the principal photographs I was, in fact, unmounted, letting Castania stand on her own, mounting only for those photographs in which I wished to demonstrate a definite point. Normally, with a double or Pelham, it is usual to use plain reins, but in my case, since my accident, this is quite impossible as my grip has been affected and I can no longer hold ordinary reins; the reins in these photographs may therefore be of interest to some readers. Being determined to ride and jump again I had them specially made for me. They are narrow and very supple, and being plaited, lock one against the other. In this way I can now hold even a strong horse safely. They have worked wonders and I can heartily recommend them to any rider with impaired grip in their hands. I would not be without them now.

We now come to the last group, the ever-popular Pelham. The fitting for this type of bit is the same as for a snaffle. The most widely used of these bits is probably what in the old days was called the half-moon and is now known as mullen-mouth Pelham (fig. 176). It will be noticed that the curb chain passes outside the snaffle ring and then through it to the other side. The object of this is to reduce the risk of chaffing and pinching, common faults with a Pelham.

Castania's mouth is, in fact, far too long for a Pelham (figs. 177 and 178). On using both reins simultaneously, the curb chain has risen up out of the curb groove and come into action on her jaw bones instead. Only when the curb rein is used alone can the curb chain work correctly for then the bit becomes just an ordinary curb. In these photographs, Castania has raised her head to the correct height, but is unable to flex properly; instead she has produced what I call a "Pelham neck", i.e. long under-neck muscles, and shortened crest ones. The head becomes set against the poll and not flexed from it as it should be. Compare these photographs with the one in a double (fig. 175). If they don't do this, they tend to over bend with their heads in against their chests, getting right behind their bits altogether.

Castania was most co-operative, but her neck is now too well muscled to show the neck to the best advantage, but the effect is there and in the old days, when she first came to me, before she had matured, it was only too painfully noticeable! Two other points to note from these photographs, the extreme tongue pressure from a mullen-mouth, and how close the bit has gone to her back teeth. Castania is not a pony suited to a Pelham, but will go fairly well in a vulcanite mouthpiece, which is much fatter and not so sharp. But she tends to pull much more in this bit than in a double, as it confuses her.

Another well-known Pelham is the Scamperdale (fig. 179), made famous by Sam Marsh and called after his place in Kent. The bent back arms of the mouthpiece prevent any rubbing, and it is an excellent bit for a horse with a sore or damaged mouth. Made in metal or vulcanite, the latter is best, but here again, if fitted properly, it is too high in the mouth for the curb chain to work and it promptly rises up out of the groove (fig. 180). For this reason, unless the horse has a very short mouth, I prefer to use it as a snaffle and minus the curb chain; as such it is excellent for a bruised mouth and a very useful bit. In either form it is one of the few Pelhams worthy of a place in a tack room. It is equally bad to fit a Pelham too low, it will get caught and rattle against the teeth, causing extreme annoyance to the horse. They must be fitted correctly.

Another Pelham of merit is the Kimblewick (fig. 181), imported from Spain as a jumping bit by the Olivers, after whose village it is called. Until recently it was made only with a Cambridge mouth, but now it is available with a jointed one as well. In its original and true form, it has its uses and suits a fairly large number of jumpers and children's ponies that need something stronger than a snaffle, but whose riders are happier with one bit and one rein; this is made possible by the fact that instead of two rings for the reins there is only a large Dee. Its action with low hands is that of a curb and with normal hands, a snaffle. They cannot combine, as in other forms of Pelhams, and herein lies its sense. It is a strongish bit and should not be treated roughly, but used with respect like a double. Used roughly it could cause damage like any other curb bit. The square eye in place of the usual round one gives it more poll pressure and therefore a greater head lowering effect. All the same it is a bit that a child, providing it is made to realize what kind of bit it is using, can do little harm with and gain greater control over its pony.

Moving now to the other end of the scale we come to an extremely harsh Pelham, the Swales 3-in-1 (fig. 182). Built on the Wilson principle of inner loose rings to take the bridle head, while the main part of the bit takes the reins, it differs from a true

Wilson by the fact that the loose rings do carry a pair of reins. The curb chain is fixed, not to hooks in the accepted sense, but to pigtails which form the top of the curb cheek. The leverage is great and, coupled with a strong pinching action from the inside rings, it would stop most things. Like the Scorrier it is best left alone; it is far too sharp, and no bit for a novice or a child.

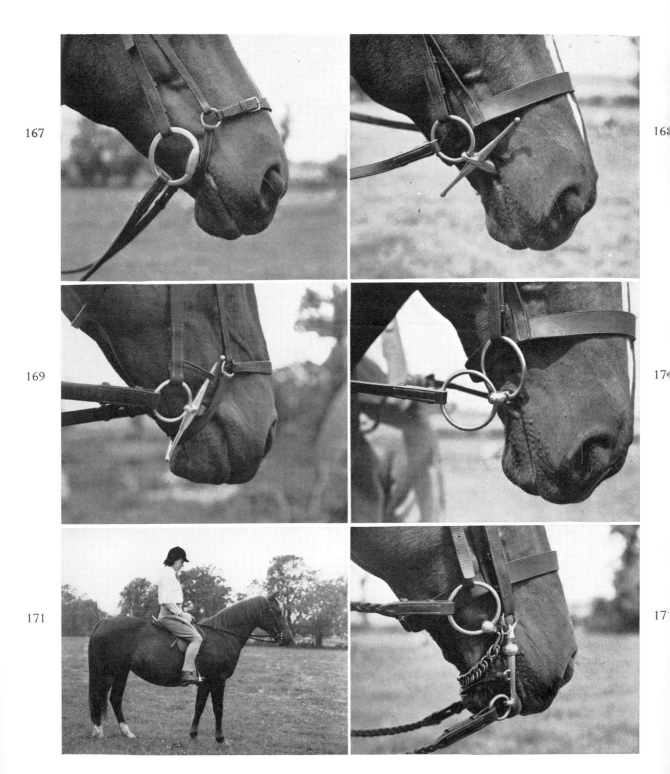

Fig. 167. Adjustable drop noseband and egg-butt snaffle (26).

Fig. 169. Fulmer complete with keepers.

Fig. 171. A comfortably fitting double.

Fig. 168. Fulmer snaffle, loose.

Fig. 170. Scorrier.

Fig. 172. Short-cheek slide-mouth Weymouth and wire-ring bridoon.

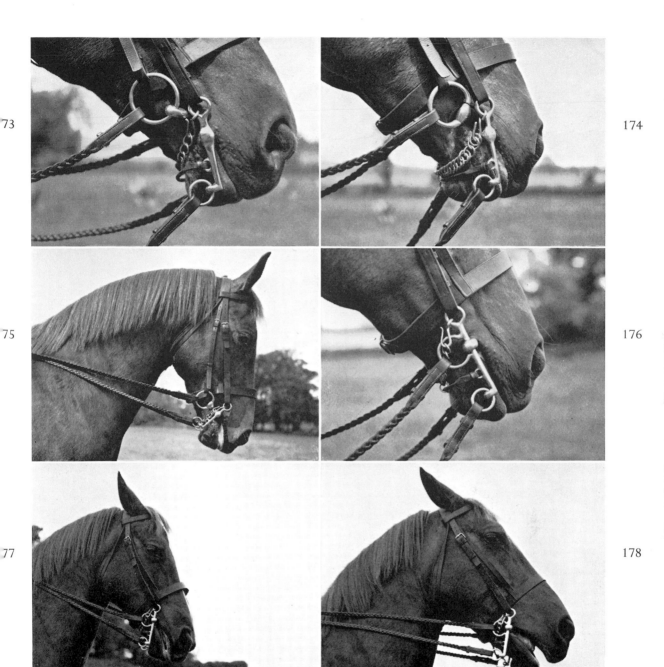

Fig. 173. Fixed-cheek Weymouth.
Fig. 175. A true head carriage (115).
Fig. 177. Showing how Castania's mouth is too long for a Pelham (25).

Fig. 174. Dressage Weymouth and eggbutt bridoon.
Fig. 176. Mullen-mouth Pelham (24).
Fig. 178. Showing how Castania's mouth is too long for a Pelham (138).

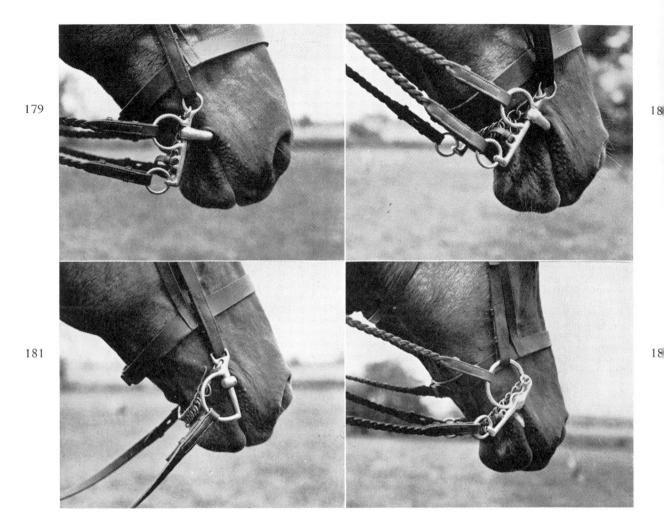

179

181

18

18

Fig. 179. Scamperdale.
Fig. 181. Kimblewick.

Fig. 180. Scamperdale showing how the chain
has risen up.
Fig. 182. Swales 3-in-1.

CHAPTER SIX

IT is one thing to see and understand what is before our own eyes. This is comparatively easy, but it is another matter altogether to visualize what lies hidden from the human eye. And bitting is no exception. To understand it, and appreciate the necessity to handle the reins with care and consideration, we must try and visualize what is going on inside our horse's mouth, for only then can we ride our horse with the tact that is required to obtain the best that he can give.

To obtain this end I decided to include X-ray evidence to help us understand. Though not easy to obtain, for it is very hard indeed to produce an X-ray that a layman can understand, and even harder to produce one that shows the points required, nevertheless, fig. 183 does show us, fairly clearly, a twisted snaffle correctly fitted. The bit in question was an ordinary stainless-steel twisted-jointed snaffle with eggbutt sides.

The horse used in the X-ray is most likely a gelding or stallion, for directly behind its front teeth can clearly be seen the tushes. On the lower jaw, lying directly behind the teeth, and in the upper jaw a matter of an inch or so towards the back teeth — cutting down the limited space in the mouth available for carrying the bit, i.e. the bars. A study of the picture shows the outline of the tongue, the bars of the mouth and the teeth, besides the fact that the bones of the nose lie a long way inside the nostrils, as we see them, proving the necessity to fit a drop noseband correctly and on no account low down, as there is nothing to take the pressure in that position. The corrugated surface of the roof of the mouth can also be seen and this, like the rest of the mouth is easily hurt and damaged, especially by a high-ported curb bit.

Turning now to the bit, the sharp nutcracker action of the joint is clearly to be seen on the tongue. This is, of course, increased when we pull on the reins, for the angle of the bit becomes more acute, and the tongue also gets trapped behind the bit. In the case of the bars, it is the part of the bit nearest the cheeks that comes in contact most, and in the case of a twisted snaffle this is normally the part with the twisting most accentuated, which is one of the reasons why the bars so often get badly damaged when a rider with either bad or rough hands uses a bit of this nature.

Having seen vaguely what goes on inside the mouth, we can now picture a little more clearly what happens each time we pull our reins, and will, I trust, make us all a little more careful and considerate towards our horses.

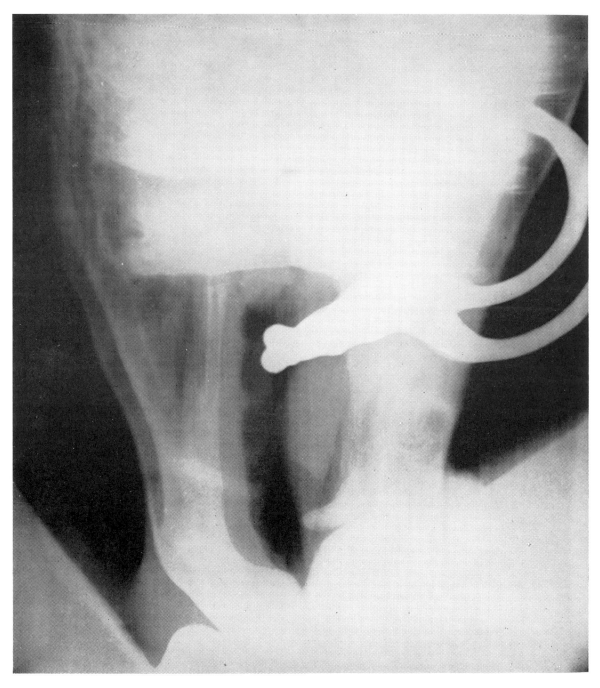

Fig. 183.

CONCLUSION

BITTING is a complex and fascinating subject which I trust this book has made a little clearer. To get the best from our horses it is a subject that must be studied, otherwise it is impossible to understand, and without understanding we can never expect to achieve a perfect harmony with our horse. But whatever bit we eventually decide to use, we must remember that no good ever came from inflicting pain on a horse, only harm that may never be undone. One thoughtless action on the part of a rider using a sharp bit can undo many hours of careful handling, and a steady, reliable horse turned into a bit-shy, headstrong ride that no one can control; who becomes a menace to himself and his rider alike, through no fault of his own. For a horse running away from pain is far more dangerous than one running away from mere high spirits, for the former is mad and has no escape from his pain, while the latter will eventually tire!

On the other hand, there is no better sight than a horse or pony comfortably bitted, be it in a snaffle, double or Pelham, enjoying life and in harmony with its rider.

In harmony with its rider.